Problems of Marriage and Sexuality Today

PROBLEMS OF MARRIAGE AND SEXUALITY TODAY

The Reverend Peter J. Riga

Exposition Press   New York

The following periodicals are gratefully acknowledged for the use of previously published material: *The Lamp, The Catholic World, Way, St. Anthony Messenger, The Priest, World Justice* and *Spiritual Life.*

73 - 155136

EXPOSITION PRESS, INC.

50 Jericho Turnpike, Jericho, New York 11753

FIRST EDITION

SBN 0-682-47638-2

For P.J.

"Vogliatemi bene, un bene piccolino,
un bene da bambino
quale a mi si conviene."

—Puccini

CONTENTS

PREFACE

It is a cliché today to say tnat the institution of marriage is hurting and that traditional Catholic sexual morality is suffering from a severe credibility gap. Confusion in these areas seems to be the order of the day.

Then why another book on this subject? For the simple reason that confusion exists! Let me clarify. It is true that the traditional Catholic sexual morality is unsatisfactory today, not because it is morality but because it is traditional. In other words, many of the conclusions of traditional Catholic sexual morality are correct—i.e., the wrongness of fornication and adultery, the stability and unicity of marriage, the evil of abortion, etc.—but for the wrong reasons. We have discovered that human sexuality is much more pervasive and important than the ancients thought or knew. Modern psychology has shown us even more clearly that sexuality affects the whole human person in all of his/her dimensions of human existence. It has also underlined with even more vigor the importance of love in interpersonal relationships, which itself is the death blow to all forms of modern playboyism. But this is only the beginning of our discussion.

What follows is an honest attempt to rethink some aspects of traditional Catholic sexual morality in light of the new insights and new needs which human sexuality has taken on in our day. It does not and cannot hope to cope with them all. Moreover, the ones which are in fact dealt with in the following pages are done so in a popular way so as to stimulate the thinking of the average Christian as he is buffeted about in a sea of sexual uncertainty. One would be a fool to think that any one book or any one author could possibly solve all these problems. The truth of the matter is that there are no "answers" to these difficult questions; only insights and directions. The individual cannot be relieved of responsibility in thinking about and acting on these questions in the light of his individual conscience.

The book is divided into two sections. The first section is given over to the question of marriage and the problems which this institution faces today. Never has monogynous marriage faced the dangers and divisions which it is undergoing today. Perhaps the greatest pastoral challenge for the Church today— aside from the question of war and peace—is that of the family. Thus we treat the questions of the sacramental mystery of marriage as a Christian sacrament, the future of the nuclear family, how to strengthen family life, and finally, the thorny questions of when marriage fails.

The second section of our study tries to grapple with special sexually oriented questions such as the so-called "new" sexual morality, abortion, overpopulation, women's liberation and the Gospel, and obscenity. Each of these questions is a book unto itself, so the most we can hope to give are some insights and tentative solutions to some very complex sexual problems.

We do hope that the following pages will afford some enlightenment to the serious reader as he individually endeavors to come to grips with these thorny problems. Herein he can hope to find no solutions but rather some insight for his own reflection. The consequent action is always his responsibility, which no book, no Church, no theologian can substitute for.

INTRODUCTION:
The Demands of Love

Before we can speak of family life and sexuality, we must first of all investigate the meaning of love itself in both its human and divine dimensions. It is this dynamic of human existence which informs and gives meaning to all human action; and since human sexual activity is an important human activity, it can have no human meaning or significance outside the context of love itself. It is, therefore, terribly important at the very outset of our study to understand the meaning and demands of love which will underlie the whole discussion on marriage and human sexuality which is to follow.

Nothing more is asked of us as Christians than that we be Christians; that is, followers of him who said that his unique commandment for his disciples was that "they love one another" exactly as he loved them. Everything else in the Christian life would flow from this fundamental engagement of the Christian; equally, if this engagement is absent in his life, then all the other ritual, commandments, obligations, etc., become worse than meaningless; they become a lie of what we do not live as we pronounce it with our lips. Since charity forms the very heart and substance of the Christian message, it becomes supremely important that we realize what it means.

Perhaps we ought to avoid the use of the word "love" in our discussion since the word has become desecrated by the world. We "love" apple pie as we "love" to go to the movies. Indeed, love has become synonymous with sex so that "to make love" is to have sexual intercourse. The scene has become so confused that many people in our society do not know how to love, so they have substituted sex and call it "love." As we shall see, sex without love is a desecration of the human person no matter who engages in it; sex is but one instrument for promoting and deepening love; it is by no means the only, or indeed the most important means. The materialistic, hedonistic, and sensate society we live in constantly confuses these ends and means; that is why there is so little love in most marriages even amidst so much sex. Therefore, to avoid this confusion let us use the New Testament word for love, which is charity *(agape)*. We immediately notice from even a cursory reading of the texts of the New Testament that there are not two words for charity: one for God, the other for man. There is only one—"agape." This is remarkable because if this is true, we cannot separate our love of God from our love of our fellowman. They are both to be loved with the very same love. This charity has come down from the heart of God, has become manifested in the incarnation, life, death, and resurrection of his son, which is communicated to us, creating a *koinonia* or communion of life with us, thus making of us one brotherhood, one Church, one communion of life and love within the very life and communion of the Holy Trinity itself. This is what charity or agape means in the New Testament. It is God's total gift of himself to men, for "God is Love" (I John 4:7), and whereby he establishes the bonds of the divine communion with all those who accept him and believe in him. Men are, therefore, radically brothers in him and form one *koinonia* with God and with each other. That is why the New Testament tells us that there is only one charity, in which and by which we love both God and the brother. Therefore, to love the brother is a form of worship, a giving glory to God, for it is God's gift to us which enables us to love the brother in this way. If at any time of our earthly existence we wish to know how we stand with God, we have only to know how we stand with our brothers, wife, husband, parents, relatives, friends, employer, employee, etc. As we love them, we love Christ, for there is no other way of loving God in the temporal existence which is ours. No one can see God; we can see him only in the face of those who confront us each day of the week. Our Lord tells us this very clearly in the sermon on the mount:

You have heard it said, "You shall love your neighbor and hate your enemy." But I say to you, love your enemies and pray for those who persecute you so that you may be sons of your Father who is in heaven; for he makes his sun rise on the evil and on the good, and sends rain on the just and on the unjust. For if you love those who love you, what reward have you? Do not even sinners do the same? And if you salute only your brothers, what more are you doing than the others? Do not even the gentiles do the same? You therefore must be perfect as your heavenly Father is perfect. (Matt. 5:43-48)

Christ tells us that the heavenly Father is perfect because he loves and continues to love all—good and evil. This love is radically different from simple human love which tends to love those who are like ourselves or who are close to ourselves (e.g. wife, family, relatives, friends). Divine charity is God's gift to men, which causes them to be like himself insofar as it permits them to act and do as God acts and does: love all, even enemies and those who reject and hate us. We can see very clearly how different this charity is from simple human love, how much more embracing, all-encompassing, and total. Therefore, one is a son of God to the degree and only to the degree that he loves as God loves, that is, with agape toward all, enemies included.

It should now be clear what makes the Christian religion unique among the religions of the whole world. Other religions such as Islam, Judaism, etc., are based principally on the love of God and obedience to his will (this is the meaning of "Islam"). Christianity is the only religion which places love of brother on the same level with the love of God. It would seem like blasphemy to these other religions since man is not on a par with God. But the Christian religion is predicated on the Word made flesh, who, after his resurrection, is now mystically but really identified with all of his brothers:

Amen I say to you, as long as you have done it to one of these, the least of my brothers, you have also done it to me. (Matt. 25:40)

After his resurrection Christ is no longer visibly present among his brothers, for the glorified Christ is beyond the categories of time and space in which we mortal beings live out our existence. Therefore, the only way we can now see and love Jesus Christ is in the face and love of our brothers, with whom the resurrected Christ is mystically united by the bonds of charity. Christ has not left us orphans; he is still in our midst by the Eucharist but also in the presence of our brothers. This becomes very clear when we examine the last words of the resurrected Christ to the apostles in the Gospel of Matthew:

All authority is given to me in heaven and on earth; Go therefore and make disciples of all nations, baptizing them in the name of the Father and of the Son and of the Holy Spirit, teaching them to observe all that I have commanded you; and lo, I am with you always, to the close of the age. (Matt. 28:18-20)

The authority *(exousia)* with which the resurrected Christ invests the Church is the power to love. This love is universal and all-encompassing, shown to all men in the life-death-resurrection of Jesus. The disciples have the mission to spread this love, this life communion with the Father, Son, and Holy Spirit, to all men of every nation and every race. They are to form the "Church," understood in its most radical signification as those men and women of every race, color, and nation who love and believe in the resurrected Lord and who are taken up into the very life and love of the Holy Trinity. The commandment of Jesus is one: love one another as he has loved us. It is in these brothers that he is now visible and present to his Church since in the Gospel of Matthew there is no ascension of Christ; he is simply present to his Church all days in the love relationship of the brothers—even to the very end of time. Indeed, when there is true love (no matter what the name of the person who loves) there is the Church, for there is the brotherhood with Christ:

God is love, and he who abides in love abides in God and God abides in him (I John 4:18).

And since we cannot see God, we must love the brothers, for that is the only way we can love God:

> No man has even seen God; if we love one another, God abides in us and his love is perfected in us (I John 4:12).

For the only commandment which we have from Jesus is fraternal love:

> And this commandment we have from him, that he who loves God should love his brother also (I John 4:21).

The result is clear: we cannot have the one without the other and, indeed, it is only in loving the brother that we can come to love God:

> If anyone says he loves God and hates his brother, he is a liar; for he who does not love his brother whom he has seen, cannot love God whom he has not seen (I John 4:20).

This is why it is so important to listen carefully to God's word preached to us each Sunday. We must not only listen to God's word with our ears but *hear* that word with our hearts. For only the man who is totally receptive to God's word is capable not of simply listening but also of hearing what it has to say to us. For the word of God is not a dead letter which was written and spoken like any other book: it is living and efficacious in our lives now as it was two thousand years ago because it is the same Spirit who lives in those words then when they were written and now when they are announced to us. There are all types of people who come to church each Sunday as explained by our Lord in the parable concerning the sower who went out to sow his seed (the word of God).

There is first of all the person who comes perhaps for superstitious or cultural reasons; or perhaps because coming to church on Sunday is expected of him by his neighbors or his children. While the word is being announced, he spends his time thinking about his golf game or his business. He spends his time thinking

about what is being prepared to eat today or tomorrow, or thinking about some problem that has come up during the week—
everything except listening and being receptive to the word of
God that is being announced. For it is the word of God that is
coming to us and we must make the effort to listen and hear.
This type of person goes away absolutely no better than when he
came into the church.

> And as he sowed, some seeds fell along the path, and the
> birds came and devoured them (Matt. 13:4).

The second type of Christian is the person who praises the
preacher: "Oh, what a beautiful sermon." This person can give
you everything that was said; can discuss, perhaps a little theologically, what was said. Generally, however, this is a sentimental
reaction—an emotional outburst for the time—but the word
takes no effect because one confuses understanding with practice.
Such a person never actually gets around to obey what the word
really says. There is some receptivity in such a person but the
will to practice that word is almost totally absent.

The third person is, perhaps, the most serious of all. It is that
person who listens, who is very intelligent, who knows exactly
what the preacher is talking about but who does not dare give
it heed. He knows if he gave it heed and obedience, he would
have to change his life; he would have to change his attitude
toward life and living as well as his mental constructs. This would
be such a painful thing, for he is very satisfied with his life as it
is. He is very satisfied with the seeking of goods or power or
prestige or position so that if the word of God were taken seriously, he would have to change. If he changed, he would encounter suffering and the contradiction of the world in which
he lives. So he hears the word but it is voluntarily excluded. This
is the third type of Christian and his condition is the most serious
of all. He rejects the word of Christ:

> When persecution or tribulation arises on account of the
> word, immediately he falls away (Matt. 13:21).

The fourth type is, of course, the ground upon which the seed comes and the person listens. That is, the person who sees himself in the Gospel message. When a parable is given regarding the good Samaritan, do we see ourselves? Are we the Samaritan loving all who are in pain or need? Or are we the Levite or priest who simply passes by? We usually see someone else; or we think of our enemy, "Oh yes, there is Mr. Jones. He is the kind of fellow who would pass by." We do not usually consider that it is ourselves of whom our Lord is speaking. We cannot concede that these words, as given by the preacher and announced in the Word of God, are actually directed to us, speaking to us as Christ spoke them to the Jews long ago. If we cannot understand that it is to us that Jesus is speaking, then we are like the other three types of persons: we have ceased hearing the word of God. If we apply the word to ourselves, we fulfill the word of Christ:

This is he who hears the word of God and understands it; he indeed bears fruit . . . (Matt. 13:23).

It is this word of love which the Church announces to us by giving us this text from Paul, the apostle. It is supremely important that we listen to this word of love for upon it is built the whole structure of the Christian religion. Indeed, the question of love is the whole question of the mystery of the human person, because it is the mystery of God himself. "God is love," says St. John. This is the only place in the whole of Scripture in which something is said positively of God as he is. It is the only statement we have concerning who God is. Every other name we have in the word of God tells us of his actions for men, in saving men. Only this one sentence, three words, "God is love," in the whole of the New Testament tell us who God is, and God is love. We cannot imagine who God is since we have never seen God. He is beyond everything we can name him to be; he is beyond all titles, beyond all we can possibly conceive. But the one title, concept, idea—love—attains God in a somewhat true and real sense. And because we are made in the image and likeness of God, love is our very existence, our very reality of who and what we are, our constitution as human beings. We exist only to the extent that we love since God brought us into existence through his love and for no other reason. So that when we reach love, we reach the profoundest and most mysterious depths of the human person, because we have reached the profoundest and most mysterious depths of who God is. The Gospels continuously speak of love.

Our Lord's commission to the apostles, the authority of the apostles, the authority of the Church resides not in domination, as the president or the congress or the law-enforcement agencies can dominate people—the law of the Gospel is love. That is why Jesus warns the apostles just before he gives them their commission that their whole attitude must be like his; that is, to serve the brothers out of love. Any other attitude completely distorts the Gospel message.

> You know that the rulers of the gentiles lord it over them, and their great men exercise authority over them. It shall not be so among you; but whoever would be great among you must be your servant, and whoever would be first among you must be your slave; even as the Son of Man came not to be served but to serve, and to give his life as a ransom for many (Matt. 20:25-28).

Their commission is to serve with love and only this. The Church cannot force anyone. The Church cannot use means to force anyone to believe or to love. This must come from the depths of the human person. Excommunications, interdicts, and other such punishments are so many unbiblical things that have come from the Middle Ages, not from the Gospels. The Gospels know only one authority and one norm: the measure of love, to teach people to love, to serve people in love. Our Lord told the apostles they would convert the world, not by teaching people to love God, but by teaching them to love one another. "See," said Tertullian in the third century, "how these Christians love one another!" He was converted by this sign of love and became one of the greatest doctors and writers of the early Church. Christianity was not and cannot be spread by argument nor by philosophy. It was spread by the fact that the Christian community exemplified within its own life the way and the meaning of love. Other people seeing that, saw the miracle of Jesus Christ in their midst. Most men hate each other, use each other, exploit each other, maim and kill each other, while God alone loves man always and unreservedly. This living of love in the community is the miracle of Jesus Christ. It is the miracle of the Christian community whereby they are known as the disciples of Jesus. They are recognized as his disciples, not that they practice a specific sexual morality, not that they obey a canon law, not that they keep certain commandments, not that they practice such and such a ritual, but that they love one another. The essential Gospel message is that we are loved by God, that he sent his Son as a sign of this love, that we are called in one communion with the Trinity and one brotherhood in Christ: one *koinonia,* one communion, one whole family of love. If Christians do not believe this, they must not believe that they are Christians. It is the simple word of Jesus.

Notice how our Lord appears after the resurrection. In each of the narratives, our Lord appears as someone else. For instance, on the way to Emmaus, he appears as a stranger: "Their eyes were covered so that they did know him." On the shores of Tiberias in the twenty-first chapter of St. John's Gospel, the resurrected Christ appears as a cook, one who is cooking fish for the disciples. And to Mary Magdalene, who is crying outside the tomb, he appears as a gardener: "Lord, if you know where they have placed his body, tell me so I may go get it." It is noteworthy that after the resurrection, Jesus is associated with his disciples to such a degree that they see him in a gardener, in a stranger, in a cook. The lesson is clear: after the resurrection, Christ has become so much identified with his disciples that what we do to one another, we do to Christ.

If we ever want to smile at Christ, we have only to smile at our neighbor. If we ever want to know our position vis-a-vis God, we have only to examine our conscience: what is our position vis-a-vis my neighbor? My wife? My employer? We must not desecrate communion, coming up to the altar for a ritualistic thing while having in our heart a grudge, an antipathy, a hatred against some neighbor, some person we know; because the food only travels into our stomach and is thrown into the sewer. It is not spiritual food for us, because we cannot communicate with Christ as long as we have hate in our heart for the brother. Communion does us no good whatever in this case because we reject Christ in our brother.

> So if you are offering your gift at the altar, and there remember that your brother has something against you, leave your gift there before the altar and go; first be reconciled with your brother, and then come and offer your gift (Matt. 5:23).

Christianity is the only religion, of all the five major religions that include three billion people of the world, that makes the second commandment the first. "You shall love God with your whole heart and you shall love your neighbor as you love yourself." It is the only religion that places love of brother on a par with love of God. The fact is that the love of God can be very illusory. "Oh, I love God." So said the crusaders as they slaughtered the Mohammedans. "Oh, I love God." So said the German soldiers as they crashed over the borders of innocent nations. "Oh, I love God." So said the Roman Catholics and Protestants as they killed each other in the sixteenth and seventeenth centuries in religious wars. "Oh, I love God." So said the Greek Orthodox and Roman Catholics as they exchanged blows for hundreds of years. "God wills it." So said religious people all through the ages as they killed, maimed, and persecuted millions of human beings. Love of God is illusory, but love of man is not illusory. We know exactly where we stand with God when we know whom we love and whom we hate. So the love of God and the love of man in the New Testament is on a par. The practice of either one is proof that the other is present. Christianity is the only religion that does this. The commandment to love the brother is the essential distinction between Christianity and every other religion: Islam, Judaism, Hinduism, Buddhism, Shintoism—all of them, without distinction. Mark Twain put it very well once. He said, "Everyone here on earth whether he is Catholic, Protestant, Jew, all want to go to heaven. But here on earth, they can't stand each other." Do they know what they are saying? In heaven, they will be as one community, but here they can't stand each other! What kind of heaven would this be? Does not this attitude and practice bring disdain and hatred on organized religion when it is charaterized by racial hatred and prejudice? Does this not destroy the very essence of what we are as Christians? How much scandal is given to the world by the lack of love in organized religion and among Christians!

St. Paul tells us all about this love relationship in his Epistle to the Corinthians. He characterizes and describes this essential virtue of charity, or love. "If I were to speak with the language of men and angels, but have not charity, I would be like a noisy gong or clanging cymbal." Perhaps preachers ought to take note of this text. Those who think that they preach so well or announce the word so well somehow come to think that they are not obliged to listen to the word. The preacher could have his audience crying in the aisles, but it does not have charity—what good would his preaching be for himself? Is is nothing; it becomes a condemnation for him. St. Paul says it is like a noisy gong which sounds for a moment and then becomes nothing.

"Moreover, if I were to have the gift of glossolalia or the ability to speak tongues, I am no better than a noisemaker if I did not have charity. If I were to have prophecy and knowledge of history and faith sufficient to move mountains, but did not have charity, I would be nothing." That is to say that if I were a Ph.D., had the most brilliant computerized mind, an IQ of 175 and did not have love in its use, it is nothing. If I have all this without charity, then I am nothing, for an existence is worth only its charity.

One exists to the degree that he loves, not because of what he knows. To have knowledge or faith enough to move mountains is not in itself a valuable thing for the Christian. It is for that reason we have and use that knowledge. Our talents were given to us, as St. Paul explains, not for ourselves, but for the brother. You want to be a doctor? Good! Wonderful! How are you going to use that ability? Like so many doctors today—in order to make a lot of money, which is a corruption of talent? Or will it be used because you love people and want to serve and help them? You want to be a teacher? Wonderful! But why? If it is only because a teacher has respect in the community or because an M.D. has position and prestige, then you are corrupt. You are not a Christian. If you want to be a teacher because you want to illuminate people in the ways of truth and carry them on to the great mystery of who they are and where they are going, then you will be a great teacher. It all depends on the intention. But what motivates that intention for a Christian is and must be love. Anything else is a corruption.

"If I were to distribute all my riches to the poor, even give my body over to be burned and have not charity, it would profit me nothing." Once again, poverty and charity do not coincide. Such acts can be done for reasons other than charity. One can give because of what other people might think or one can share for motives of pride and prestige. Only we can see, and God can see. Even if I give everything I have to the poor and become a pauper in rags, but give from a motive of pride or esteem for the eyes of others, it would profit me nothing. One can go as far as to give everything, even one's body into slavery, in order to free another (as was done in the time of St. Paul) and if this were done for any motive other than charity, it would be as nothing before God.

In Verse 4 of the Epistle to the Corinthians begins the positive elements of charity. "Charity is patient and kind." The two words are biblical and go back to the Old Testament. "Charity is patient." That is to say, it is that quality which is long-suffering. Charity forgives enemies and injustice even when one has been unjustly offended or rejected, even then, the man of charity forgives. One forgives his enemies. This forgiveness is the characteristic of love. This is phenomenal because it is the hardest thing for man to do. Humanly speaking, it is impossible to do, and that is why charity is a divine gift in that what we are incapable of doing, with God's gift of charity we can do it. Indeed, this quality of long-suffering and forgiveness is the very quality which both the Old and New Testaments attribute to God. That is why charity is necessary as God's gift to man for him to do what is humanly impossible: to truly forgive enemies and those who hate and wish us harm. We say we forgive, but deep down in our hearts we seldom forgive our brothers. The husband who has been unfaithful is continually reminded of this for the next fifteen or twenty years because his wife never ceases to bring it up in order to humiliate him. We do not forgive, since we repeat the words only with our lips. To forgive is to blot out, really and truly, this evil action as though it no longer existed and is no longer taken into consideration. Certainly, the memory is there; one cannot erase that. But it is no longer taken into consideration in our dealings with that person. That is how God acts toward men. Because we are called to be like God, we are called to do the impossible, humanly speaking, because it is God's grace of charity that has been given to us since charity is a divine gift, not a human trait. This is why we can do the impossible act of forgiving enemies. We have so absorbed the mentality of the world that we hate what the world hates—the North Vietnamese, the Vietcong—just as much and to the same degree as the people around us. What are *your* attitudes toward the Chinese and the Russians? Among most Catholics I have met, there is a wealth of hatred of people, second to none. It is the spirit of the world crushing us, against which the charitable person is patient and strong. "My grace is sufficient to you."

Charity is kind—kind, meaning pity. One is moved to forgive because others are weak human beings like ourselves. We who have been the object of pity and forgiveness in God's mercy must imitate God as dear sons: "Be merciful as your heavenly Father is merciful." In the Gospel of Luke, mercy is love. That is what St. Luke means when he says: "Be loving as your heavenly Father is loving." One of the chief characteristics of charity is that we are moved to mercy: mercy for our brother's weakness, whoever he may be: wife, husband, children, neighbor. We are moved by pity to forgive them all. Here it is God who is our exemplar, and we follow his example because we are his sons. "Be sons of your Father," says Jesus in the Sermon on the Mount, "that you might be like your Father who causes his sun to shine on the just and unjust and the rain to drop on the good and the evil." God loves all men, even sinners and ingrates. He continues to love even when they offend and reject him. He does not cast them off because "they are hopeless." Therefore, true charity is always kind toward all men because all men are loved by God, and Christians are his sons precisely in this charity.

"Charity is not jealous; it is not pretentious." How many airs men put on to impress others! How much more intelligent we are than so-and-so! How much richer we are! How much better house we live in! Pretentious and boastful! The fact is that God has given us talents and goods—these are good—but how do we use them, once again? Boastfully? For our own aggrandizement? If this is the case, our charity is jealous and pretentious. The desire to affirm oneself in one's eyes before others is a great temptation. A person can even be vexed to see another doing good and will try to do more to show his own goodness. Charity however is not pretentious. Pretentiousness is illusion. Charity and truth go together just as egoism and illusion go together. Any charity which seeks glory is a false charity.

"Charity is not self-seeking, nor does it selfishly consider its own good." That is, love gives. And the more I give, the more I love in a disinterested way, expecting nothing in return. To that degree do I grow as a human being. People often tell me, "Well, Father, that person doesn't return my love; therefore, why should I love him?" The reason is simple: because we are sons of God, and we must love like God, who continues to love even when people no longer love him. He is like the mother who cannot forget the fruit of her womb. The child can live without the mother, but the mother cannot live without the child. She is listening and hearing and thinking of him all the time. This is beautifully put in the Book of Deuteronomy: "I have graven you upon my palm, so that you are always before my face." God cannot forget because God always loves, and that is what we are called upon to do— not seeking our own good, but the good of the people we love.

"Charity does not think evil, it does not rejoice over injustice, but concelebrates with the truth." Charity always thinks the best of people, not the worst; it is the cynic who, because he has been hurt at one time or another in love or has been rejected, now says that love is no longer possible. This is a truly cynical attitude, and it is a sin against charity. If an injustice is done even to our enemy, true charity doe not rejoice. Last year when the Chinese were forced to buy grain from Canada, some Christians actually rejoiced at this misfortune. Why? Because our enemies were shown to be, in a sense, inferior to our productive system. What kind of charitable thinking is that, that to "prove our point" we must watch millions of people go hungry? This attitude is the way of the world. This attitude is the brainwashing of nationalism —not the charity of Jesus Christ.

Charity rejoices in the truth, in all goodness and justice no matter who does it or the name of the man who does it. When a man—any man—brings about more justice, more peace, more compassion, more mutual understanding among men, this is a work of Jesus Christ because it is a work of love for brotherhood. Even if such a person does not bear the name of Christian or perhaps does not even believe in God, he unconsciously seeks God because he consciously seeks love; and who abides in love, abides also in God and God in him. The Christian who truly loves, rejoices in this goodness and truth no matter where it is found.

"Charity suffers all things, endures all things." Love suffers all things. The word used here for "suffer" is the same word Christ used in his passion; namely, that love continues even if one is rejected. The charitable man absorbs that hatred of other men into his own heart and refuses to strike back in violence. Love and nonviolence are intimately related everywhere in the New Testament. The man who is violent is not a man of charity and love. Charity bears up against all adversity. Thus it demands constancy and strength. Strength in Christianity is not manifested by violence. Charity that is not ready to suffer is not complete or mature.

Thus, the man of charity is like the Lamb of God, Jesus, who absorbs hatred rather than strike back at his unjust accusers and tormentors. His absorption of hatred on the cross becomes the liberation of men and their freedom to love. We are called to imitate him. Is it not strange that when we talk about the philosophy of the world and nonviolence, we have so absorbed this attitude that we praise the man who can kill, but the man who refuses to kill, the conscientious objector, we disdain and hate. This is a sign of terrible corruption, even in the Christian community. The Gospel often speaks of nonviolence, but the man who takes it seriously and refuses to kill by becoming a

C.O. is considered some kind of queer, or a radical and a fanatic. It is strange because the Gospel teaching is just the opposite of this philosophy of the world.

"Charity believes all things, hopes all things, endures all things because charity never ceases." True charity believes a person can do better. When we tell our children that we have confidence in them, we love them, we expect more of them, we want them to do more and we want them to do better. Why? Because we love them. Love ceases when we do not believe or expect good things of those we love and the reason for all this, St. Paul says, is because charity never ceases. God is love, as we said at the very beginning, and because we are made in his image and likeness, love is our whole existence.

Charity is always ready to believe and hope in the best. Charity can never renounce fidelity because God never renounces his. From a human point of view we have many reasons for dis- trusting others and losing hope. But the Christian in charity can never do this because God never abandons men no matter how evil and seemingly hopeless they are. God's love continually goes out to the little ones, the wicked, the evil, the sinners. Charity does not say all men are good; only that it loves and continues to love in spite of their evil. To the degree that we do not love, we do not exist. That is why the man who lives now in love has the beginning of eternal life, because he exists in God, he participates in God's own being. And the man who refuses and goes by the hatred of the world, such a man is closed in upon himself and he has begun to experience, in the profoundest sense of the word, *hell,* because he does not love.

God does not punish. God does not throw anyone into the fiery furnace with sulphur pits and screaming people and all other forms of mythology that we have constructed for ourselves. God does not punish. It is man who so inhibits himself from loving, who has grown so cold to others in mercy and pity that he is incapable of inhabiting with God for eternity, for God is love. The man who refuses to love has begun even now his eternal death. The man who refuses to love below refuses in eternity to love. He has created and begun his own hell now—in the *now,* to be continued and consummated in eternity. So the man who refuses to live with his brother, who refuses to respect him, to help him, to hope in him, to believe in him, to pity him, that man is living in his own hell. Here is the perfect theological definition of hell without the mythology of devils. Theologically speaking, the foundation of man's being is love. It is the mystery of love because it is the mystery of God, and man is made in the image and likeness of God. So that if we refuse to love, we refuse God himself. But if we are open, now, to begin to receive, to forgive and to have pity and to have mercy, to share with others, we will begin to open ourselves to God because we are open to love.

But charity also hopes in others against all appearances to the contrary. One never really gives up hope for a change in the one whom one loves no matter what condition he is now in. Charity does not give up hope because to the very end of a man's life, God continues to love perfectly and unceasingly. It is this divine charity within us which will never permit us to give up hope for even the greatest of sinners.

"When I was a youth, I spoke as a youth; I understood as a youth; I thought as a youth. But now that I am a man, I have grown out of my youth. For we see now in a glass darkly, but then we shall see face to face. Now I know only in part, but then I shall know even as I am known." This is like a mother and a baby. All a baby knows is "Give me, give me, give me." It is natural to the baby because it is an infant. But when the baby grows up to be a true mature human being, a Christian, he begins to give love, and then he receives maturity of his humanity and his Christianity. "Now that I am a man, I have grown out of my youth."

"So there remains faith, hope, and charity, these three, but Why? Because faith and hope are a vision, an expectation of what is to come. But the expectation of faith and hope is God, and in charity we attain the essence of who God is. So that being like God, charity in our own lives will live forever in eternal life; is now ours and will be for all eternity, for God is love. If we abide in love we abide in the dimension of eternal life, even now. The man who abides in charity, therefore, has eternal life because he has God. There can be no other mode of existence for the Christian.

Part I
MARRIAGE AS INSTITUTION
AND REALITY TODAY

I THE MEANING
OF HUMAN SEXUALITY

In any serious discussion of marriage and sexual problems today, the very first thing to be investigated is the meaning of human sexuality itself in its phenomenological as well as religious context. This chapter is written in the form of a list of the various aspects of human sexuality. The list is not complete but it does represent some phenomenological and religious observations on the question of human sexuality, its development as well as its inner meaning.

1. The biblical teaching on human sexuality is both blunt and beautiful. In Genesis 1:26-28 and 2:18-24, we have the clear teaching that marriage is both an institution for the propagation of the human race as well as a mutual and loving relationship between a man and a woman. It is within this loving, sexually oriented relationship which is marriage that children are to be born as products of that love. Thus man as a sexual being is created in the image and likeness of God because he is a creator with and by love. Love and procreation within the text of Genesis are essential if we are to understand the statement that man has been created in the image and likeness of God.

In the New Testament (Eph. 5:21-23), the sacred institution of marriage is elevated to a sacramental level in that this human love, already present from creation, is itself now made the symbol and moment of a greater reality, the love which continually exists between Christ and the Church. It is in the very act of loving in all of its human dimensions (which in marriage, includes above all as a sign of love, sexual relations) that the couple as a unit of love increase in their love of God. Human love here is the very moment and possibility of the divine love itself. Sexuality in marriage is not "alongside of" the "spiritual" but an integral and essential part of the divine-human reality which is the sacrament of matrimony.

31

2. Yet, the historical Christian view of sexuality has been ambiguous. Western civilization has been infected by a crypto-Manichaeism which has made matter—and above all the sexual relationship—an evil, if not in fact at least as a "grave temptation of the flesh." To the Christian spirit, which sees all things as created and redeemed in Christ (John 1:2-6), it should be evident that there is nothing which is evil except what man by his perversity has made evil. When the Bible speaks of "flesh" it does not mean "matter"; it means simply man in his totality as a weak being completely dependent upon God for all things. To identify the biblical "flesh" with "matter" is to profess the very first Christian heresy against which our Creed reacted: "God is the creator of all things, visible and invisible."

3. The great amount of eroticism on display in American life betokens a form of moral escape. Our society needs titillation because it needs to escape by the use of alcohol and the massive drug culture. But escape from what? It needs to escape from the consciousness of its own mortality and from the inevitable dread of human existence, which is death.

No person can understand human existence until he faces the inevitable reality of death in his own life, honestly and calmly so that, thereby, he can return to himself in order to give a meaning to his human existence—and human meaning is impossible without love. For man's basic drive is not that of sexuality, as some Freudians would have us believe, but a will to meaning and significance. When men no longer have meaning in their lives, when they despair of the meaning of their own existence, then some escape must be found in order to forget or numb the deepest frustration and pain of our persons: despair. It is then normal for individuals—indeed for a whole society—to seek oblivion in the deep instincts of the emotions, such as eroticism and tittilation at every level: entertainment, literature, cinema, theatre, friendships, advertisements, human relationships, etc.

Historically, every society which has been overconcerned with eroticism in its public and private life, was a corroding and despairing society, despairing of its own meaning in history. In this, then, the increasing presence of eroticism and pornography should evoke sadness much more than anger, awakening much more than indignation. What is needed is education of sexuality within the context of love at every level, not crusades against smut.

4. Another observation concerning the education to human sexuality is that human sexuality appears as a human reality which is essentially relational and, at the human level, can only be interpersonal and intersubjective; that is, a relationship between persons. Any other view of sexuality is a perversion; that is, a use of persons treated as means instead of ends. Human sexuality, then, can only find its true meaning in love. Sexuality does not produce love (even though it can nurture and strengthen love) but rather love employs sexuality to express itself incarnationally, making of sexuality a specific and unique language of love. Human sexuality then is always a means at the service of love.

Thus sexuality draws a man and a woman out of his or her isolation. In inferior species of animals, reproduction is brought about by breakage and multiplication. Sexual dimorphism introduces a greater possibility of diversification, selection, and mutation. In man, sexual dimorphism appears as a stage of a process of amorization, that is, as a true lovemaking. At the level of the couple, sexuality is the bearer of personal and social communication. There is no personal encounter—that is, an encounter of persons—in the copulation of other animals since the animal exists only for the species. When two human persons encounter each other, it is they who forge a union that sexuality can express or confirm but cannot create. That is, once again, sexuality comes to express, confirm, and solidify an interpersonal love relationship and not vice versa. Sexuality is man's opening and possibility of gift to the other in love, for it is only by love that we can touch another human person.

5. Man can refuse to go out of himself to the other. He can become the "playboy" who uses others (or they use him). The name "playboy" is singularly appropriate: when we use others, we have not grown up emotionally but remain at an infantile stage of development. To be fully human, sexuality must be seen as man's opening to persons and therefore to love. Eroticism is the negation of love and lust becomes the end of one's spirit.

Eroticism is a sort of blockage of human development and therefore a perversion.

Love for the other even to the point of sacrifice of self is alone truly human, but the "we" created by this love is always fragile. This love always vacillates between history and the instant moment, between liberty and fatality. Man can thus redescend to the animal level and enclose himself in an indefinite repetition of sexual acts leading nowhere, or he can choose the continuity of a human presence (love). This latter choice is one of a communal history in which this sexual act is a privileged moment in the continuing growth of love. For love is properly the history of a mutual personalization, confirmed, strengthened, and made more profound by repeated sexual activity. This is what we call the personal and personalizing oath to love which is perennial and strong as death. We reach then the final efflorescence of human sexuality in what is known as marriage. We shall come back to this specific aspect of Christian sex education which is based squarely on the reality of human love.

6. It is difficult, if not impossible, to define sexuality. What we do know from various phenomenological studies is that each human being possesses himself in a sexual way relative to another human being of the opposite sex and that the comprehension himself—herself as being-as-man and being-as-woman is comprehensible only within the context of the man-woman relationship. But as anthropologists have pointed out time and again, this relationship is relative to particular time and culture and it is not possible to set up any one "ideal" of sexual, conjugal, or familial relationship to which being-man and being-woman should conform.

On the other hand, promiscuity is a mark of the animal kingdom, not of man. Specificity of sexual relationship to another human person is the human characteristic of man's sexuality. Of all the higher vertebrates, man alone has an absolute rule of prohibition (i.e., incest). This is indicative of the fact that man's biological nature with all of its force is subservient to man's cultural nature and serves human ends. This is unknown among the animals, even those animals closest to man such as monkeys, chimpanzees, and gorillas. This universal rule among men clearly establishes and distinguishes a natural process from a cultural one. Human sexuality as distinguished from every other form of sexuality, is a personal growth and a history, not an animalistic repetition of the same phenomenon which the milieu and/or glands so dictate, common among all other forms of animals.

7. This view of sexuality, it must be further noted, is a complete turnabout from the traditional moral theology view of human sexuality, which has been based now for hundreds of years on precisely a sort of sacral biology and naturalism. In reality, what this moral theology has been from the time of St. Augustine is a refusal to take human sexuality seriously both in its human development as well as in its total expression. What this means is that human sexuality takes a man beyond himself to another human person. Human sexuality is always transcendent to biology or simply to the continuation of the species. The relationship of masculinity and femininity is the concrete manifestation, in a particular culture, of the transcendence of the human person. What is primary in man is not sexuality but a personal relationship of encounter and need of another human person. Man and woman discover who they are in their encounter *with each other for each other*. It is this relationship which renders man's biological corporality human, and therefore cultural as well.

Thus, at bottom, human sexuality is not determined principally by biology but by a human relationship within a particular culture, which the individual's biology must come to implement and serve. It is love—the highest evolution of the relationship between the sexes—which reveals to each sex that the one is made in function of the other as a totality.

Consequently, the meaning of sexuality is not a given (as is the case with the animals) but a human task to be accomplished which cannot be found "in man's nature" but in the interaction of persons. Otherwise man is made an object who slavishly follows "his nature" instead of being a subject who actively creates and fashions his world. It is precisely in regulating and controlling his biology for human ends that man becomes subject *of* (not to) his own destiny. We can see here how profoundly incorrect is the view of "natural biology" as the basis of human sexuality. In such a biological view, man's body is seen as an instrument

which must be used according to its own finality, which man
must slavishly follow but never direct (the view of *Humanae
Vitae*).

On the contrary, sexuality is given in human life not just for
the species but it belongs above all to each person's being in the
world and to others with whom he comes into relationship. It is
true that we can lie with our bodies, that is, where the symbol of
love does not translate the reality and substance of our inner
meaning (sexual abuses in their various forms), but this form
and exercise of corporality ceases to be human to the degree that
it fails to establish a truly human communication whose perfect
accomplishment is human love.

8. There is, however, yet another dimension of human sexuality which must be recognized if healthy sex education is to be
complete. It is that of the child who comes to break the enclosed
circle of the two sexes in their mutual relationship. It is the child
which comes as a safeguard against egoism *a deux* and which
directs the couple outward to encompass the wider community in
its own love. It is the child which makes the demand of love by
its very presence and which obliges the couple to truly manifest
themselves as a "we" to society. It is for that reason that Christian tradition always saw childbearing not just as procreation but
as education as well, two moments of the same loving act. Sexuality then demands of its very nature a life-giving process to
others, and thus the child is not to be seen as a sort of "accident"
to conjugal love but as its epitome and efflorescence. The child
comes from the very inner meaning of human sexuality itself.
The sexual relationship is, if we wish to use religious terminology,
a creative act in a perfect sense, since it is creative not only
socially and culturally but imminently to the couple in love. They
have this creative power in the power of their love. It is a participation of the creative love of God himself. It is safe to say
that any human sexuality deprived of the experience of maternity
or paternity remains incomplete, and adults become truly adults,
paradoxically only in and through the education of children with all
that entails of labor, effort, sacrifice, love, tenderness, discipline,
and detachment. Therefore human sexuality is not only a communication between the couple but is also a communication be-

tween the couple and their children, and beyond, to the larger society of mankind. Thus human sexuality is not only an inter-subjective relationship but a trans-subjective relationship as well, since from the union of the couple, autonomous persons arise.

What is above all else necessary in any form of healthy sex education is the promotion—in the couple and in the family—of the values of love, opening to life and care for others, of participating in the establishment of a more just and human society both at home and around the world. As Rollo May put it so beautifully: "We receive love . . . not in proportion to our demands or sacrifices or needs, but roughly in proportion to our own capacity to love. And our capacity to love depends in turn, upon our prior capacity to be persons in our own right. To love means, essentially, to give."

II THE SACRAMENT OF MARRIAGE

After the discussion on human sexuality comes the sacramental reality of marriage itself. Human sexuality, as we have seen, is essentially relational in nature, that is, it is related to two poles, masculine and feminine, for its basic meaning. This mutuality or polarity, however, reaches its efflorescence in a mutual gift or commitment of one human person to the other. This commitment given in love is what we call marriage.

Marriage, therefore, is always incarnational and symbolic in the sense that the mutual love of the couple comes to express itself by means of signs and symbols, the greatest of which is the body. It is precisely this incarnational vehicle which must be understood in order to understand the Christian notion of marriage as a sacrament. In the following chapter we shall endeavor to grapple with this mystery and reality.

From the earliest days of her tradition, the Church was conscious of the special reality of Christian marriage (cf. Matt. 5:27; Mark 10:11; Luke 16:18; Cor. 7:39; Eph 5:18). Christian marriage (or marriage in Christ, as it was called), was certainly all that any human marriage was among the pagans, but it was, however, to be more profound insofar as it symbolized the Church itself in miniature form; and because it symbolized a moment of divine love and grace among men, it was from the earliest days considered to be what today we call a "sacrament." But how?

Most of Christ's teaching on marriage (Matt. 19:9) referred directly to the text of Genesis 3:16, where marriage is seen to be a holy thing, something natural to man and created by God. Marriage is a reality so profound in man's mortal existence that he will leave every other relationship in order to become part of this fundamental community. The teaching of Genesis on marriage is at once nuanced and beautiful, where man cannot be defined or understood except in function of woman and vice versa. Adam's nature is the measure of Eve's nature (and vice versa) with the result that it is the couple which is the sacred reality created by God for man. Marriage, therefore, of its very

38

nature, is a holy and natural state from the very creation of man himself.

The second text that had a great influence on the early Christians with regard to their thinking on marriage was Ephesians 5:21-33. In this text, St. Paul sees a marriage as a sacred reality because it reflects and symbolizes the marriage (or love) of Christ with the Church. The reality of marriage is based upon and is supposed to reflect this union and love of Christ for the Church. Marriage is in this way a supernatural event where the mutual love expressed between the couple (in all of its dimensions) is of itself elevated to (and is a participation in) the very love which Christ has for the Church. This as yet has not told us how marriage in the Christian dispensation is a true sacrament.

In the order of God's mind and plan for the redemption of man, it is the Incarnation of Christ which is primary. Because of God's love and for no other reason, the Word became flesh to show men God's love and the way to God's love in visible and tangible form. Jesus is the historical revelation of God's love for man in visible appearance:

And the Word became flesh and dwelt among us; and we saw his glory, the glory of the Only Begotten Son, full of grace and truth. (John 1:14)

By this very fact, because the Word becomes one race with humanity, the Church is born out of love. The whole life of Christ—from his incarnation to his glorious death and resurrection—was (and remains always in and through the Church) the visible manifestation of God's love for men (the Church). This fundamental reality of God's love and mercy is the radical basis for the redemption of men. Christ, and following him, the Church, are the fundamental sacraments of God's victorious grace in history.

Marriage as a sacrament stands within this reality of love and mercy in time. The love which the partners have for each other is a participation, an actualization here and now of the love of Christ for his Church. For the community which is established by the joining of this man and this woman, is a Church in miniature; and when they love each other, they become the sign and symbol of the divine reality of love in their lives, thus constituting, not an empty symbol, but a truly efficacious one which we call a sacrament. The attitude and relation of Christ to the Church is the radical model of love for the attitude and relation which must be brought about in the reality of marriage, since Christians objectively represent this love of God in Christ for the Church.

It is at this point that it is important to understand exactly what is the Christian reality of love, the heart of the redemptive and conjugal reality we are discussing. We have seen that a sacrament is the visible and historical manifestation of God's grace to man. Yet, the very heart of both the redemption and the mystery of human existence is the mystery of love itself, which is God (1 John 3:8). Human love and divine love are not two generically different realities, but one reality. Indeed human love exists because it participates in the divine love. Love is man's opening to God in time (and in eternity whose beginning is in time) as well as the very event of God's loving communication with man, which we call grace.

In marriage, two human beings open themselves to each other only in and through love and become a loving "we." Married love is thus the actual practice of love of man (these two human beings) in giving each other to each other, in suffering with and for each other, in the death of selfishness and egoism, striving to live a human and loving existence together amidst all the vicissitudes and joys of life. Marriage thus represents and symbolizes in its way (by love) the redemptive and loving act which Christ had (and has in the Church) for the Church. Christian marriage is thus a miniature humanity, and therefore a miniature Church, wherein men love and sacrifice for each other out of love. The very unity and reality of marriage is love for each other—which symbolizes and brings about the Church's function among men. Each Christian marriage is a sacrament precisely because it is a miniature Church in which the historical realization of the Church's unity takes place, that is, in loving one another. Any marriage, but more particularly Christian marriage, then, can never be simply a "secular" reality because its substance is love and the event of love and grace which not only unites men and God but man with his fellow man. Each Christian couple is a sign and symbol of love, which expresses the deeper and underlying reality of the loving union of God and man. In marriage, the Church becomes present in this tiny community of redeemed mankind.

It is in this way that we can say that marriage is a sacrament. When two Christians, /a free man and woman, consent to love each other forever in agony and in joy, which characterizes all of human existence, this mutual love becomes an actualizing symbol and sign of the Church in history, and the Church is thereby actualized in her essential loving function in *this* couple at *this* moment of redemptive history in their loving one another. The reason is clear: in loving each other for better or for worse, in sickness and in health, for all days, they in fact contribute to the union of Christ with humanity; i.e., in this little community of humanity at this precise moment in history. In their human love which opens to divine love, marriage creates the existence of the whole Church in miniature fashion as the grace-giving presence of God in history. Marriage is therefore a symbol and a sign, but because it is based and created by love (when this is present), it is an efficacious symbol of God's merciful love-grace in history. The sign and what is symbolized are therefore united in marriage, but they must not be confused since we know that the sign can be an empty sign in marriage; that is, when there is no longer any more love in forming that marriage, what is symbolized is empty of meaning. Therefore, we can say truthfully that the Church is present in marriage but only to the degree that the marriage actually realizes its own nature of loving communion, a loving "we" of redeemed humanity; that is, when the marriage is sanctified by grace and lived in holiness. Thus the sacramental sign of marriage can be said to be the visible bond of ultimate, indissoluble love between the partners until death, and what it symbolizes is true love and holiness lived in Christ, which actualizes redemptive truth in this portion of redeemed humanity here and now. Christian couples, therefore, by living a holy married life, by that very reality, participate in a salvific function. Marriage is therefore holy in its origins but only because it received its fullest expression and culmination in the redemptive will of God in the marriage of Christ with humanity by and through the Incarnation. Marriage brings two people into the mystery of redemption and for that reason can be called a sacrament.

This love within marriage also, by its very nature, opens the couple to the world in redemptive relationship. It is here that we meet the reality of the family as the natural expression and outcome of the love of the couple themselves. The begetting and education of children is the first encounter of this redemptive love of the couple with the world. As a continuation and incarnation of this love (sexual relations), the love itself becomes expression in the world by and in children and the family. This relationship of love to the world is so vital that even when it is not possible for a particular couple (e.g., age or infertility) this function must remain open to other outlets in the expansion of love. For the nature of marital love has also as one of its essential functions to open this couple to others, whether to children of their own or to other people. When this love is thereby communicated to the world, the sign itself of marriage is all the more intensified and growing. The sacrament of marriage is then open to the world; that is, as a sign of redemptive love to and for others. The very nature of true marital love should lead the couple from themselves as a loving "we" to the communication of love to others (family, the world). In this way, marital love should not and cannot become an enclosed community (couple plus children) but an opening, of and by love, to the larger community of the Church.

III THE NUCLEAR FAMILY TODAY

*The nuclear family as we know it today is not a very old pheno-
menon as far as human institutions go. There is, therefore, nothing
sacred or sacrosanct in this reality. As we shall develop here, the
present structure of family life is undergoing a stress from which
it might well not be able to recover except by undergoing a
whole new metamorphosis. Both affluence and a radical critique
of present family life by women's liberation is bringing about this
new thinking on the mode and expression of family life today.*

The modern family faces a whole multiplicity of problems
today. These problems are so great that many experts have
already predicted the early demise of the family as an institution
of stability and child-rearing.

Perhaps they are right, and they will be right unless we
examine closely the reasons for the present *malaise* of family life.
No one should be so foolish as to say that the reasons for this are
few or that they can be reduced to a specific number. They are
indeed many, about which we must consult a variety of people
and professions for help.

But I should like to discuss two important problems of family
life which, in my opinion, are deeply at the root of this malaise:
the whole concept of the nuclear family today and the flight from
children, as demanded by the articulate professional feminists. To
examine these two questions is to examine some of the deepest
roots of our present dislocation of family life.

If we rapidly examine a short history of marriage, we see
that through the ages we have had what we call the patriarchial
type of family. The family was not simply husband, wife, and
children, but was the extended family. The patriarchial family
included the various generations which encompasssed grand-
mothers, grandfathers, aunts, uncles, etc., all living under the
same "roof." This was the nomadic ideal, which lasted right up
until the nineteenth century and, as such, was the ideal of family

life. The fact of today's familial reality is that this view of family
life has radically changed. The nuclear family is the family of
today which includes mother, father, children—and these only.
This new situation of family life has advantages but it also has
great disadvantages. As a result of this evolution a nuclear family
is no longer dependent on the extended emotional support of many
people, such as upon grandmother, grandfather, aunts, uncles.
Finally, the family is more dependent for its psychological and
emotional fulfillment on each other; for these reasons, the
sexual love between the partners becomes even more important
today, even crucial. This is so because it is only in this personal
and personalizing area where he or she can, in this very impersonal and bureaucratized world, become himself and herself.
The family is the only place where he or she is truly important
and indispensable. This person loves *me,* I can find my psychological equilibrium within *this* nuclear family since we live in a
world that is almost completely permeated by bureaucratic
impersonalization.

It is clear then how the emotionality of personal sexual love is
so vital and important to the individual emotional and psychological equilibrum of the partners, and, conversely, how fragile
family life is today.

Moreover, the element of mobility of today's family life has
created terrible rootlessness, alienations, and loneliness in the
nuclear family. The average family in the United States lives in
one place something like eighteen months. We are a nation
continuously on the move. The company calls and men go. A
man roots up his family and he moves everything out. This has
advantages. Indeed, because of high mobility, a family can pick
its own friends, its own line of work, its own recreation and
community. All this is a great advantage, but it also has great
disadvantages. The fact is that in California, the most mobile of
all the states in the union because it is the most technologically
advanced, we have one out of five adults on a prescription
tranquilizer-depressant drug. It has something like five hundred
thousand alcoholics, and more than one out of three marriages
ends in divorce. This is not to mention the many unhappy
marriages which, somehow, manage to stay together. Something

is wrong with the nuclear family, but hard empirical evidence is not present in this crucial area.

This poses some interesting questions for those of us who have thought that the nuclear family of the twentieth century is a moral ideal. This was the unwritten premise of the *Moynihan Report* on the condition of minority, mostly black, families in the United States. Since many black families have a disproportionate number of one-parent (mostly female) families, family life itself among these groups, concluded the report, was in jeopardy. This is hotly disputed by many sociologists.

And rightly so. It was industrial life which necessitated the present nuclear family and created the breakage of the extended family which had been the norm of family life since the dawn of recorded history. The modern industrial state necessitated the nuclear family because of manpower demands which, in its own turn, demanded small family units so as not to drain away vital— and limited— financial resources. It was a functional family life, but functional not for the family but for modern industrial life.

Already sociologists are beginning to discover that children reared in such homes are less successful in coping with the reality of human existence than children of extended families. If this evidence increases—as it seems to be doing—the moral ideal of nuclear family shall have to be radically rethought and new modes of family life fostered and encouraged.

Moreover, as mentioned above, there is less scholarly evidence that the nuclear family of the twentieth century is an historical fluke and that to survive as human beings, we shall have to return to variant forms of extended families once again. What else can be concluded except the failure of the nuclear family when we see and hear the cries of boredom, aimlessness, and discontent that children raised in such homes during an era of unparalleled affluence are making? The present values of modern American nuclear families cannot withstand the onslaught of aimlessness and disintegration of human relationships brought about by the false values for which nuclear families became nuclear families: material advancement. This was the cause of the nuclear family and it is this which has become its demise.

There is, corresponding to this, a whole ground swell of

communalism arising throughout the country on the part of many young people (and sometimes, not-so-young people). There is a deep yearning to find some kind of more intimate human and familial human association which will eliminate the sense of privateness and fixed role embodied in the small isolated family. The young long for the richness of human relationships which comes from extended family life. The poor extended families examined by Moynihan might well turn out to be the moral norm and the nuclear family, the historical freak. This richness of human association, which was cut by the industrial revolution, may well be the answer to our profoundly disturbed youth today. It seems more and more evident that the nuclear family is simply incapable of surviving as a viable, vital institution under conditions of economic stability and affluence.

There remains, of course, the difficult question of finding such viable forms of extended family life today under present economic conditions. But the difficulties are perhaps not as great as we might imagine. The nineteenth and early twentieth centuries demand by modern industrialization that families be small and therefore nuclear, is rapidly undergoing a dramatic change. In an ironic sense, it is precisely the technology of the industrial period which may yet be able to free us from the familial slaveries of the past. Automation and cybernation are rendering work, as we have known it, obsolete and regressive. We are being freed more and more from the "jobs" associated with material stability. It is precisely cybernation which can free us from economic—and therefore, familial—slavery and isolation, to permit us to search for more human and fulfilling roles in life. The young have already begun this search precisely because they know 1) they are not needed as a labor force; 2) the material values and goals of the nineteenth- and early twentieth-century families, which gave them cohesion and a sense of purpose, is unsatisfying from a human point of view; 3) human relationships are the supreme values of human existence and these cannot be nutured in isolation but in extended familial community.

What forms these communities will take it is not given for the theologian or anyone else to say. What we can say is that the evolution back to more primitive, extended familial relationships, has already begun and is not a passing fad. The young have too much history on their side.

There is another sign of the degeneracy of family life today in the new demand by women's liberation: a flight from children. It is a demand to be free of children, who are seen to be a burden to "women's full development as persons."

This demand itself is in function of a more fatal flaw in these professional feminists, and that is that the art of child-rearing has lost its goals and moral values. Middle-class Americans once had a clear set of goals and values which they belived in and lived by: hard work, thrift, self-discipline and mostly, in function of material acquisition. For various reasons, the young have lost confidence in these values and yet have not been able to replace them with any other values. What comes after you have the fine house, two cars, a boat, color TV, etc., etc.? No new goals or values grew up to replace the old. Parents now have nothing of real value to impart to their children. So, the upbringing of children has become not just "permissive (this is too facile an explanation) but rather *laissez-faire,* which any day-care center can impart. Having no clear idea what values they wanted to transmit or what goals they wanted their children to reach, intelligent women began to find motherhood and child-bearing a bore. The professional feminists have only articulated what is implicit in these attitudes: if you do not see motherhood and child-rearing as the supreme art of value-imparting and goal-communication—man's greatest work—then it is a bore to be escaped from at any cost, even when financial circumstances do not require the mother to do so. Thus follows the inevitable downgrading and deprecation of motherhood itself and the ubiquitous call for universal day-care centers as a "right" of every and all women even when economic necessity does not force women to take up work. Without lived values and spiritual goals in life as inculcated in family life, then these professional feminists are correct in pawning off children to a day-care center. Any center can feed, clothe, "teach" children, and keep them from physical harm. But no child-care center can impart a set of spiritual and moral values which make life human and worth living. This can happen only in families.

It also follows that the moral values for which parents stand as a family are supremely important for their children. The drug addict problem among the young people, experts have found time and time again, comes principally from the fact of a weak father image, of broken homes, of weak family life at home, or from parents who professed certain moral values but lived another. When the family stands for inferior values such as money, prestige, etc., the situation is dangerous for the future of family life itself. In *The Road to H,* Dr. Isidor Chein says that 90 percent of all those drug addicts he has investigated (and through the years he has investigated thousands) come from broken homes that had no great moral values, or where the mother and father stand for nothing except materialistic and social values. In other words, parents must incarnate in their own lives what they stand for, because their children mimic them from the day they put them to the breast. Children imitate parents almost perfectly and they absorb their moral values with the milk they drink. Freud, if he has shown anything, has shown that this earliest influence of parents on their children is all important. So the values, moral and spiritual, parents want their children to have, must be practiced by what they do in their own lives. It is the old adage of the preacher-practitioner; that is, one must be what he says he is or children will call parents what they call them today—phony, inauthentic, liars. These words signify for the young the elders who say one thing and yet practice another. They see clearly, for instance, that parents who say they live for brotherhood and believe in love and at the same time discriminate against people because of race, color, and creed, are living shallow and inauthentic lives. If there is one thing we can no longer do with the sophisticated children of the last third of the twentieth century, it is that we can no longer lead empty, valu-less, and inauthentic lives. When the family no longer fulfills the basic function of spiritual and moral value-impartation, then it must disintegrate for it has no *raison d'etre.* Its soul has died and the radical feminists are correct in relegating its function to day-care centers.

As William Shannon has put it so well "We can refuse to

have children. But if we do have them, we cannot abdicate our role in shaping their future. We cannot evade a crisis in adult values by adopting a *laissez-faire* attitude toward the young. Our flight from children is but a flight from ourselves and our moral confusion. Their unhappiness is a mirror of our own."

IV STRENGTHENING FAMILY LIFE TODAY

The stress and strain on family life today is making itself felt in many ways: broken and unhappy marriages, alcoholism, extra-marital affairs, mental breakdowns, etc. It seems more and more evident that the average family left to its own resources is incapable of responding adequately to this stress and strain. Means must be found to cope with this great pastoral problem of our day. This chapter will be spent in discussing ways in which this can be done.

Without being either a Cassandra of doom on the one hand or a naive optimist on the other, one can say that family life today is going through a terrible crisis at every level. This is true because society at every level is going through a terrible crisis because of change. We have had more change in the last sixty years (it is now a cliché to say) than mankind has experienced in all of its past history, written and unwritten, from the time he came out of his primitive caves up to the turn of the twentieth century. As we shall see, these radical changes at every level of living have and will continue to have a deep effect on man's family life and his image of what family life can or should be. This is not necessarily bad, but it does mean that family life today is facing problems which it never had to face at any time in its former history.

When we speak of family life from a Christian perspective, we must speak of it, of course, in the light of God's word, but we must also speak of it in the light of the word of man; that is, in the light of psychology, anthropology, sociology, and other human sciences which over the past twenty years, have given up a fantastic insight into our own prejudices and errors of the past and which, in this period of crisis, tension, and change, can perhaps lead us to a more stable view of married life, as well as to a truer view of family life than we have had in the past.

The past, we can see today, has bequeathed us a great many prejudices. For instance, St. Thomas Aquinas calls woman an "imperfect male" *(mas occasionatus)*. This only reflects the type of tradition we have received, which saw with a jaundiced and prejudiced eye the relationship between man and woman. The Scripture's teaching, with regard to marriage and with regard to the sexes, of man's consciousness of himself as male and woman's consciousness of herself as female, is very simple in the Book of Genesis. This scriptural consciousness is one of unity of man and woman as one whole: the couple. The teaching of Scripture is very interesting. It does not contain any of the prejudices of the male-orientated society which has come down to us from tradition, both Christian and non-Christian. Its teaching is simply that man and woman find their self-identity and their own meaning in function of the other, that both together make up a couple and appear before God as a couple. Scripture, when it speaks of *man,* does not speak of the male sex; it speaks of the couple: "male and female, He made them, and they became one flesh" as Scripture says when Adam is lonely. In this myth-ical way, the Scripture puts the fact that man exists sexually: male or man, female or woman; that is, each is essentially a half being, that in order to find the fullness of his being, each must appeal and must relate himself to the opposite sex to find his own self-identity. That is why Adam shouts with joy when he sees Eve—"and this is bone of my bone and flesh of my flesh, and this is why she shall be called *woman,* because she is taken from man." This shows clearly the basic equality between these two beings and not simply equality, but Adam in that mythical story of Genesis, finds his own self-consciousness in this essential encounter with woman. He finds the loneliness he had experi-enced broken because he has found some one similar to himself, someone who is his equal, and this he could not find in all the rest of the animals that he had named. He found none like himself, but woman he found like himself and he realized him-self as man *only* when woman came into being. So the teaching of Scripture is very nuanced and very beautiful. The basic equality, but much more profound than that, the basic con-sciousness of man as male and the basic consciousness of woman as female comes from the *relationship* of man and woman. This will have great consequences for the rest of our study.

The Babylonians had another type of myth that showed this basic unity of the two sexes. The early Assyrian pagan religions of the Near East, from which, of course, Judaism originally came (Abraham came from Ur of the Chaldees), had another view. They say man was a basic sexual unity but they did not say, as Genesis said, that woman was taken from a rib. *Rib* in Hebrew and Arabic means the closest possible companion. If you are my rib, you are my closest friend. The Babylonians had another view. Their myth was that the creator-god, *Mardock,* took man, whom he made as one, and cut him in two. He cut him into two sexes and each part is always and perpetually looking for the other because they are both one complete unity. Both of them are basically incomplete and without the other they are essentially lost and empty. The teaching of the Scripture is therefore very simple. The prejudices of the male society that, for instance, somehow or other something is basically "natural" to woman as woman, and somehow or other something is basically "natural" to man as man is simply not contained in Scripture. What is contained in Scripture is the basic equality, the basic unity, the basic relationship and consciousness of love between male and female. That is all. There is none of the prejudices of "the eternal woman," or the "passivity and the activity" of the sexes, the "receptor and the giver," and other types of analogies between the sexes that tradition and history have conjured up for us.

It does not take much study to also see that, historically, the only permanent relationship between the sexes that anthropologists have been able to see—that is, the only relationship in which man distinguishes his sexuality from that of all the other animals in family life—is the basic concept of incest. There are certain women who are forbidden to certain men. That is to say, a sexual relationship between mother and son, between father and daughter: the father may not marry his daughter and the mother may not marry her son. This is not true of any other animal, including monkeys, chimpanzees, baboons, and apes, who are anatomically very close to man. Given the proper conditions, the female will copulate with her offspring in order to continue the species. But only man has had this universal prohibition in every culture throughout the world and through human history. From this one prohibition have come all the rules and regulations about marriage, because man is more than his sexuality. Man controls his sexuality for certain ends. This is to say that man *has* his sexuality whereas the animals *are* their sexuality. Man is a being who is transcendent to any and all of his drives and instincts, and controls and directs them in function of human goals.

Various cultures have developed the man-woman relationship in various ways. Margaret Mead, for instance, in her anthropological studies of the Samoan natives of the South Pacific Islands, has shown various tribes in which biologically the woman, of course, has babies, but where every other function is different. After birth, the woman leaves the baby immediately to be taken care of by the male. She goes out and works all day and comes back at night while the male develops the home life. The male even begins to develop very soft muscles, very weak and sensitive type of skin, whereas the woman develops very strong muscle and skin due to the work in the fields.

These modern anthropological studies clearly show that we must not try to put forth various types of myths that "woman's place is this" or "man's place is that." One simply cannot prove this from any cultural or anthropological study, nor can one prove it from the Scriptures. The only thing one can show historically is that man has tended to dominate woman and to keep her in a socially inferior position and place. The male's own sexual image today has come from the fact that in various ways he has dominated woman and that this has shown that he was "better" than woman. This is nothing more than a sexual racism: since the woman is different from the male, man is somehow superior to woman; it is the same type of reasoning that some people give with regard to racial discrimination. "Since the Negro has a different type nose or mouth or color, he must be inferior. Obviously that's true, isn't it?" That is scientifically as well as morally ridiculous. On any objective test, the Negro's intelligence might be different, but the Negro is absolutely in no way inferior to the white man. So too, the same line of reasoning: since woman is different, since she has more delicate features, and since he has strong physical features, as developed in most cultures, the woman was considered to be inferior. This type of inferiority even goes so far as the Church's law. In the Canon Law of the Catholic Church, codfied in 1917, one finds that women legally are to be treated along "with children and idiots." Women are not allowed to have real property in the element of marriage: it is the man. The Code of Canon law is a code conceived and elaborated by men prejudiced by male-dominated history.

Today, of course, all this is dramatically changing, as woman takes her place in society as a human being in her own right. This new phenomenon creates a certain havoc in the male mind. Since his image of himself was in relationship to the inferiority of woman, he will now have to begin to reshape his own image of himself as woman changes the image of herself. Woman is the last bastion of prejudice, and as she begins to become herself as person and searches in a spirit of change, the male now becomes very afraid. And yet they really have no reason to be afraid at all. The riches of the development of a human being, of the female of the species, is the enrichment and the fulfillment of the male of the species. Because, as was shown above, man's consciousness of himself as male is dependent upon woman's consciousness of herself as female. Consequently, any enrichment in one or the other is precisely the enrichment of the other as an inseparable unity. There is nothing to fear, even though we must change our conceptualization and relationship between the sexes. This change is rapidly developing today.

Another important element of change in today's society is the relationship between sexual love and procreation. It is marvelous to note how in all Catholic theology theologians treated this relationship. The major question in almost nineteen hundred years of Catholic theology of marriage, from the time of St. Augustine up until the nineteenth century, is negative. The question which was asked was, "How can we justify sexual intercourse?" This starts off the basic relationship between the sexes in negative fashion. In fact, sexual intercourse does not have to be justified at all. Genesis puts it very clearly that a man's union with his wife is total: psychological, physiological, and moral. "The two shall be as one flesh." This is the expression of the total gift of one to the other: it is fulfillment, one of the other within that total gift to each other.

Historically, it is easy to see how this relationship in family life was interpreted to favor procreation of the species over the sexual union of lovemaking. The continuation of the species was always precarious at best as can be seen from the fact that famine would wipe out whole populations and that in the fourteenth century, two-thirds of Europe was wiped out by the bubonic plague. Child mortality rates were something like two out of every ten children surviving to adulthood. All of this has been so dramatically changed by the increase in vaccinations, modern medicines, better and more plentiful foods, that famine today, at least in the developed countries, is a thing of the past—with the result that the emphasis on procreation has taken second place to the emphasis of sexual love. Being a nuclear family and being no longer dependent on the extended emotional support of many people—grandmother, grandfather, aunts, uncles—and, finally, being more dependent for their psychological and emotional fulfillment on each other, the sexual love between the partners becomes ever important today, even crucial.

This is why the encyclical, *Human Life,* of Paul VI was and is such a great tragedy. The encylical takes none of these human and marital aspects into consideration; as if an encyclical on married life could be conceived by an unmarried cleric with a few advisors, out of contact with the reality and experience of marriage.

It is clear then how the emotionality of personal sexual love is so vital and important to individual emotional and psychological equilibrium; and, conversely, how fragile family life is today. Even traveling on the freeways to and from work has its influence on family life. The man has driven for an hour to get in to work, works eight hours, usually at a job that is impersonal, then drives another hour to get home. Consequently, both partenrs become "up tight" and yet the man must recognize, and almost in a sense have great discipline with himself, that his wife who is with the children all day long must have some adult conversation. The husband is the only adult she really can converse with at an adult level. Unless he can relate to her in a personal, adult, and human way, even when he does not feel like it, then the marriage will begin to lose force because communication with each other will begin to break down. This will not happen perceptibly, but over a period of five, ten, or fifteen years they will begin to see their marriage disintegrate.

All of this makes it clear that it is within this modern context that sexual love takes on the element of a language. It is *the* language between husband and wife which is not spoken simply in bed but in all of their personal and human relationships during the day, with the children, with their neighbors. The marital bed is only the clearest expression of that sexual language prepared for by the comportment of family life itself. Sexuality, then, is not simply a means for procreation, as past tradition has emphasized. Procreation is responsible today within a limited context: economically, socially, psychologically, demographically within that nuclear family. Indeed, too many children can be disastrous in such a situation. Therefore responsible parenthood is a basic necessity and duty between the couple, as they honestly, before God, see how many children they can emotionally, socially, psychologically, and demographically bring into the world. And only they and they alone can make this decision. That is why the sexual relationship between a man and his wife becomes all the more important today because it becomes that expression of human engagement and human love where "I"— the "me" who is treated like a cog down at General Motors or at Kaiser Gypsum—am important. In his family, however, each person is important as person. He and she are deeply loved and, therefore, sexual love is the relationship of a language which we must all learn, that every married couple must learn. If sexuality is not a language, if it is simply a biological function and if it has degenerated into instinct and boredom, then indeed the marriage is becoming disintegrated at its very roots—not immediately, but over the five, ten, fifteen year period. It is astonishing to note the phenomenal divorce rate among Catholics. Among Catholics, the divorce rate is much lower than among the rest of the population for the first fifteen or twenty years of marriage; but when it gets to fifteen or twenty years of marriage, the divorce rate among Catholics zooms upward beyond the normal percentage of the population in general. Why? Because these Catholics think that they must stay together "for the sake of the children." By the time they have been married fifteen or twenty years, the children have been more or less through high school or college, or are married, and the couple now feels free to go their separate ways. What they do is simply consummate by divorce what they have been doing for years: separate physically from a state in which they have been psychologically and spiritually separated due to a lack of communication, lack of language, lack of sensitivity between themselves from the very first years of their marriage.

To love another human being is perhaps the most difficult thing in the world; and for people who think that by breaking up their marriage, getting divorced, and looking on the other side of the fence for greener pastures, there is an old Chinese proverb: "He who takes a new way only finds new problems." If a person goes into marriage with a problem, he will simply have a bigger problem. If a person is immature he is going to be an utter failure, insofar as marriage is concerned. Marriage is kept together with effort at personal communication and inter-personal relationship at an ever-deepening level. When this ceases or is taken for granted, the marriage, imperceptibly, has begun to disintegrate.

Even today, however, with the mess that family life is in, we ought not be too discouraged over this picture. Young people still hold a great idea of marriage. They consider marriage as an ideal, that children are good, that married life is something worthwhile striving after. This is great hope for the future; but at the same time, these other factors which we have mentioned (alienation, as the sociologists would put it) is a basic reality and a factor which we must carefully consider, understand, and weigh in the lives of married people.

What can be done? No one has any clear-cut solutions in this period of crisis. No theologian has all the solutions. But here at least are some helps and hints at stabilizing a family life today that is at once nuclear and yet lonely.

First: Friends. We must have friends. That is, friends who share the same goals as we, because there are many people who do not share our Christian view of family life and sexual love. We must find friends with whom we can speak and live and exist with in a very profound way. Our friends will be our salvation. Thereby, the nuclear family breaks out of its loneliness by becoming more of a greater extension of community, if you wish, with those of our friends. We share problems and agonies. We share above all the goals we wish to reach in Christian marriage. That is primary for family life today.

Secondly, women should be encouraged to develop their talents and abilities—whatever they developed in school or elsewhere, such as writing, painting, poetry, nursing, teaching— commensurate with their obligations to their children, if they are under age. Her children need her, obviously, in their younger years. They suffer from great insecurity if the mother is not at home. But at the same time, some sort of cooperation between husband and wife should be possible so that she can develop and use those talents that are hers. In modern society, the wife-mother is going to spend something like thirty-five years after the "nest" has been emptied. Children are always temporary. Someone once told me, "As a priest, that must be your greatest sorrow, that you have no children." Well, it is, but for the fact that no one has children forever. When we all get to a certain age, we must lose our children or we have been bad parents. Our children are always temporary. Parents have to cut the umbilical cord and let them out on their own. That is what love and freedom mean, and when we have done that, we, too, will be lonely. What are we going to do then? Watch television for thirty-five years? That's incredible, as well as humanly absurd. We must develop those talents that God has given us, whatever they may be. It is only a male prejudice that says that woman's place is in the home. In reality, woman's place indeed is in the home with her young children, but always commensurate with her God-given right to develop herself as a human being. There are all kinds of possibilities here and with a good and understanding husband, many things can be worked out together. In this way, too, they will all share even more with each other.

Thirdly, hospitality toward friends and neighbors. Hospitality is a fundamental virtue of the New Testament that says that the

Christian must be hospitable. That is to say, his home is always open for those who are in need. He is sharing of his time, his abilities, his very life, his goods with those who are in need. It is a virtue one cannot really specify, but people know it when it exists or does not exist. How many generous people do we know at whose home we can come, open the refrigerator, and just be ourselves? Hospitality, openness toward others, sharing goods, love, and whatever one has with friends and relatives and neighbors who want to come into your home, is an important virtue in offsetting the baneful influence of loneliness and anomaly. St. Benedict had the following motto put over every Benedictine monastery: "Receive every stranger as you receive Jesus Christ." That should be the motto of every Christian home. When anyone comes to their home, they should be made to feel welcome—not the phony welcomeness, but a real heartfelt welcome as one would welcome Jesus Christ. Loneliness will then be all the less for that blessed family.

Fourthly, there is the danger to family life that can come from the fact that so many men today are caught up in their businesses and professions. I realize that every man gives himself over, to a great degree, to accomplishing goals which, today in modern society, is called business. These achievement goals, of course, are necessary for man's own self-identification. Without a "job," understood in the broadest sense of "to work," and unless a man accomplishes or creates, then indeed, that man's self-identity in the world we live in is in grave danger. The result is that the necessity of working, of professional accomplishment, of variant forms of business, understood in the broadest sense of the word, is a basic necessity for male identity and equilibrium. But the fact is that in modern society many of these business and professional accomplishments require so much time that it becomes highly dangerous for family life. Each man must examine his own conscience to find out whether he is neglecting his family or not. This absence of the male over long periods of time from the home becomes doubly dangerous with regard to young children, particularly young boys, who must have in their very early years as well as in their teen years a strong father image that they can identify and grow up with. If this is lacking, then the youngster can begin to have all sorts of psychological problems and can even lead to problems of self-identity, homosexuality, and drugs. As mentioned earlier, the fact is that modern research has discovered that when the father is either absent from family life totally, or absent to a great degree over long periods of time, this alone has a deleterious effect upon the image that the young, particularly the male, has of himself. One of the greatest weaknesses of our society is that our young males have very weak father images with the result that the female has had to supplement for what the father has not given. For a female to supply a father image in the family, either through necessity or because the father is "too busy" in his business, is to endanger completely the male self-esteem of himself, particularly the young males in the family. This must be avoided at all costs, even if it means less time "at the shop."

Fifthly, I wish to emphasize the part that parish life can play in solidifying family life. As was mentioned, the greatest weakness in family life today resides in the loneliness and rootlessness of the nuclear family. The average nuclear family, with its high rate of mobility, moves once every eighteen months and consequently suffers from loneliness, rootlessness or what the sociologists call anomaly. One of the main preoccupations and apostolates of the parish of the future must be to attempt to give some root, some warm and personal community feeling, to these families who are separated and lonely. When a family is lonely, and separated from relatives and long established friends in a community that is strange, in surroundings that are strange, precisely because of modern mobility, the family structure becomes weak and fragile.

Therefore, one of the functions of the parish of the future must be to attempt to create more human and personal relationships and community. It must be a catalyst in this regard, for it has a deep binding factor which no other community or group can possibly have: faith. Essentially, this is the whole object of what the Church is all about. The Church in the New Testament is called "The Family of God," "The People of God"—moving forward in this land of pilgrimage toward the promised land. We move forward, however, as a family and as a community;

we move forward, as the *Acts of the Apostles* tells us, as brothers and sisters together in the Church. The New Testament idea of Church is nothing more than those who have accepted, loved, and believed in the resurrected Lord Jesus, assembled around the Eucharistic table, nourished by the same food whereby and in which they become true brothers and sisters in the profoundest sense of that word. Therefore, symbolically and really, they are brothers and sisters. The realization of this reality in concrete form is the greatest necessity for the parish of the future.

Consequently, the parish must attempt, in all ways open to it, to establish this warm interpersonal relationship of community. When the parish fails to do this—and indeed up till this late date it has failed to do this with its large churches and impersonal liturgies, with its type of functionalism and sacramentalism that has been so characteristic of the Church for the last eight or nine hundred years—then the rootlessness and loneliness of family life is simply accentuated. A rootless, lonely family comes to a strange and impersonal environment, goes to a church like an auditor (even if it be a participating church in the liturgy), comes home almost as lonely as it was before. Consequently, what we need is smaller groups, smaller liturgical home groups, more home masses, more interpersonal relationship-centers of multipurpose buildings where we can get together for discussion, reading, meditation, or small liturgical services. What we need is organization block by block of places and homes in which the persons in some particular home will welcome all the brothers in that block on a regular scale, taking turns in that area so as to create what we really are—namely, the family of God—taking an interest in each other, learning to know each other, and then, when we have learned to know each other, the final result should be learning to love each other more intensely. This will intensely solidify family life in modern society.

Sixthly, what modern couples need today are periods of silence and of meditation, away from the hustle and bustle of the world they live in. Family retreats are becoming more popular, but even when it is not possible for whole families to make retreats, then it should be possible for couples to make retreats, or simply days of recollection, where they can go off with each other in order to enjoy each other, relate to each other, and discuss common problems; to meditate on what their marital existence is or should be, what their family is in relation to themselves, and consequently in relation to God. Without these periods of silence, believe it or not, communication can be entirely broken down, because only when we learn to speak to one another is there any form of communication. Where there is communication, there is knowledge, and where there is more profound knowledge, then love can grow. But when there is only hustle and bustle, when there is the feeling of being overtaken by the chores of rearing children, by job or work, etc., then at that point, perhaps suddenly or over a long period of time, communication can begin to break down. This must be avoided at all costs and the only way to really do this is to get away from the hustle and bustle of business and sometimes even of family life, in order to go together to a retreat house, or to the country alone, and there for a short while to try to relate to each other as human beings. In this way, the lines of communication will be perpetually open. This is how a couple will learn how to take and to give, to criticize, but always to criticize in love, so that those little difficulties in communication that are very small at the beginning, when noticed and paid attention to can be cured and not allowed to go on for years with the result that after five, ten, fifteen years of marriage, communication has been entirely broken down. When that happens, it is almost impossible for communication to be rebuilt.

Lastly, I would say that in every parish there should be a full-time qualified marriage counselor even if the parish has to pay the ten or fifteen thousand dollars a year for a professional man. In a day and age such as ours, when families are so fragile and so weak, when we see family life being more and more corroded from the inside and from the outside, and when we see that the preparation for marriage is so weak, such a counselor's presence is imperative. In Holy Church, for instance, before a priest can be ordained he must study long years, sometimes as long as from four to eight (after high school), before Holy Church will ordain him; on the other hand, for marriage, where there is any preparation at all required at the local level, it usually consists of a few lectures with the local pastor or the assistant pastor. For the most part even this minimum preparation isn't present in most dioceses. What we need, then, is a more intense preparation for marriage. What we need is a marriage counselor who can direct these activities in a parish.

One thing ought to be clear, that just because a man is a priest or a pastor, does not mean that he has the necessary qualifications for being a marriage counselor or for counseling married people in their difficulties. This is simply not true. This problem must be approached on a professional level by a counselor who has been trained in human relationships, the breakdown of human relationships, and who can spot these in couples having difficulties or in couples preparing for the sacred act of holy matrimony. Consequently, such a professional person must be hired by the parish. It would also be good for every couple to go to such a man every few years, make an appointment, and discuss the progress of one's marriage and the little difficulties that are cropping up. In this way, the counselor can point out, on a professional basis, what can be done in order to correct the little aspects which, if allowed to go unchecked, can grow into greater difficulties later on. In hiring such a man, the parish can put its money toward the greatest need today—strengthening family life. We go to see a doctor every few years, particularly when we get a little older; we go for a complete check-up because things tend to run down and we don't even know why or when they do. So, too, with regard to human relationships. Our relationship in marriage will be different today than it was five or ten years ago when we got married, and every five years or so it will be different again as well.

The secret of happiness, at least that modicum of happiness that is given to us here below, is to be able to grow together intelligently, emotionally, psychologically, morally, and spiritually. Great dangers arise when one person does not grow with the other in either or all of these dimensions. For it is the biblical concept that we go before God as a couple. We relate to each other essentially as man and as woman, as a couple, so that we grow together as man and as woman, as a couple. Consequently, when one or the other of the partners refuses to grow in any of these areas, then communication has already begun to break down at its most fundamental level. If this is allowed to continue, more and more alienation of one person from the other is inevitable. It must be checked at its very beginning.

CONCLUSION

In conclusion, then, after all that has already been said, it is clear that marriage and family life today are undergoing a very grave crisis. But not all is bleak; not all is hopeless. We must recognize on the one hand that to lead a profound, growing, personal, human, spiritual, and Christian family life is much more difficult today than it was fifteen, twenty, or one hundred yeas ago, precisely because the culture in which we live militates against stable marriage and family life. Yet, there is also great hope. There is great hope in the young, who still value marriage as a great human relationship, who still value children as products of love and consequences of love. Family life is still looked up to as an ideal. It is not disdained—at least, not as yet. And consequently, given all these factors that we have discussed; as well as the various helps we can give to family life, it is possible within this context to strengthen that which has been weakened and is being continuously weakened in our society. For if it is a cliché to say that the fundamental structure of society resides in the family, it is all the more true to say that the fundamental structure of the Church is also family life. Perhaps it is even truer to say that the Church *is* the family of God, in which each couple should be able to find themselves and other couples together. For we are not saved as individuals. We are saved as couples, as marriages within the one marriage of the Lamb to all men. We are not even saved as individual marriages. We are saved in conjunction with all men; as the Apocalypse puts it, it is "The bridal groom and marriage between the lamb and the whole of the human race." All of us, when we strengthen married life in whatever way we can in our own lives and in the lives of others, are doing truly the work of Jesus Christ, the blessed and expected bridegroom.

V MARRIAGE AND DIVORCE

The reality of divorce and remarriage is becoming a very familiar phenomenon in the modern world. The same can be said for Catholic marriages as well. The fact that the Church teaches that there is no such thing as divorce for Catholic Christians does not obviate the problem nor does it solve the tremendous pastoral problem which divorced, remarried Catholic Christians pose to the Church as a whole. What we desperately need in this area is some fresh rethinking of the subject in the light of the agonies which this problem poses for literally millions of Catholics in the United States. In this chapter, we will endeavor to do just that.

The question of divorce and remarriage has preoccupied the thinkers in the Church in a special way these past few years. The reason is evident: the number of divorces and those Catholics directly and indirectly touched by divorce have increased alarmingly over the past twenty years. According to such experts as V. J. Popishil who has written on the subject, there may be over six million such Catholics in the United States alone. It is reasonable to conclude then that the question of divorce and remarriage is the most pressing pastoral problem of the American Church today and will become ever more pressing in the future.

This situation has forced both theologians and canonists to go much deeper into the very reality of marriage as a Christian sacrament. Strangely, there has been very little research and thinking on this score, with the teaching of marriage remaining mostly on a juridical and legal level. What theologians have clearly seen is that this traditional way of looking at marriage as a sacrament is irrelevant and counterproductive. We must look more deeply into the very theological nature of Christian marriage as a sacrament. We can no longer live with the juridicism of the past. The testimony of young people and priests in the pastoral ministry is eloquent testimony to this fact.

The difficulty here is that this theological task remains to be done and yet there are millions of divorced Catholic people hurting. What can we do? Can a priest, in conscience, simply say to these people that it is a difficult law of God but it is nevertheless the law? This seems to be inhuman at best and irrelevant at worst. The need for a strong education in marriage has begun to be recognized by the American Church at every level. We need a more in-depth preparation for marriage; that couples must be helped to grow in their love after marriage is all true and of the greatest importance. But we must also look at the human and sinful situation as it, in fact, presents itself to us: we must also try to render spiritual assistance to those who have been unsuccessful in one marriage and need to be encouraged in their second union even if this second marriage is not properly "sacramental" but simply a situation which is humanly best for these two people. In other words, we cannot, millions of hurting people cannot wait for the theology of possible second marriages to be fully developed—something which is a long way in the future. We must attempt to exercise what the Greek Church calls the "economy of mercy" toward second marriages; that is, marriages which are not the perfect ideal of the Gospel injunction but which are humanly salvageable and salvaging for the people involved in them. It is ironic that in the question of war and peace, the Church has been traditionally satisfied with much less than the Gospel injunction of nonviolence ("the just war" theory) while, at least from the Council of Trent (1563), she has been adamant in the Gospel injunction of the ideal of indissoluble marriage.

It would be worth our while to go over some of the scriptural, theological, and sociological grounds of divorce and remarriage. We cannot hope to be complete but we will attempt to give some of the highlights of the argument. Our conclusions, then, will also be tentative since the theological, historical, scriptural, etc., developments are as yet tentative.

From a scriptural point of view, the question of the possibility of divorce and remarriage in special circumstances is problematical. In other words, the Gospel teaching on divorce and remarriage must be considered to be ambiguous and not binding. Biblical experts are simply not agreed, for instance, on the meaning of the exception contained in Matt. 19:3-12. For instance, some exegetes consider this exception given here by Christ to be a clear exception. The Jews considered a woman who committed adultery to be truly dead—therefore divorce was possible since the wife had died in the act of adultery. Not all exegetes agree with this interpretation, but what comes through most clearly is that the Gospel gives no complete teaching on marriage (and, therefore, neither on divorce and remarriage). No hard and fast injunction condemning all forms of divorce and remarriage can be found in Scripture from a strictly exegetical point of view. This is important to remember since otherwise the question would have been settled long ago among the Christian Churches. The fact that there is dispute in the interpretation of the scriptural texts—even among Catholic exegetes—shows clearly that the argument from Scripture is not conclusive but ambiguous.

The argument from the teaching of the Church condemning divorce and remarriage absolutely is not conclusive as well. Most authors cite the famous Canon 7 of the Council of Trent on marriage: "If anyone says that the Church errs when it has taught and teaches, according to the Gospel and apostolic doctrine, that the bond of marriage is not able to be dissolved by the adultery of the opposite spouse . . . let him be anathema." Catholic theologians are not in agreement on the interpretation of this passage. Men like P. F. Fransen think that the council was not thinking of defining a doctrine of faith as revealed by God but was defending the discipline of the Western Church against the reformers. The latter declared that the marriage bond could be intrinsically dissolved by the adultery of one of the spouses; what the council did not declare was that the Church did not have this power. The point might seem academic to the average person, but Church documents must be read carefully, historically, and within context. It can legitimately and theologically be maintained that the teaching of the Church has not definitively ruled out true divorce and remarriage, at least in certain cases.

All of this must be said, of course, for the future when theologians think more deeply on the sacrament of marriage and its signification in the economy of salvation. As we have said at the beginning of this chapter, no definitive conclusions can be drawn with regard to the indissolubility of Christian marriage and the Church's approach to those who in fact live in second marriages. But at the same time, there is room for further development in this area, which has not been ruled out by a definitive declaration or teaching of the Church. In other words, the indissolubility of marriage is presently a teaching of the Church, but it is not a definitive teaching of the Church and, therefore is susceptible to rethinking and modification in the light of the needs of the institution of marriage today.

All of which leads us to basic pastoral considerations—which is as far as we can go today, given the unevoluted stage of its doctrinal development. As all know, Vatican II brought no new doctrinal developments in this area in its document, *The Pastoral Constitution.* Yet, what this document did emphasize was the personalistic nature of Christian marriage; that is, the very definition of marriage itself is determined by the conjugal love existing between two persons contracting marriage. Some commentators of the council even went so far as to claim that love was the constitutive element in Christian marriage, while others deny this. In either case, the centrality of love in marriage is a definite progress away from the traditional juridical conception of marriage—which itself has vast ramifications for any future theology of marriage. For if it is true that—as some commentators of the council hold—conjugal love is the constitutive element of Christian marriage, then marriage ceases to be when love no longer exists or where, indeed, the incompatibility of the spouses actually becomes mutually destructive. Once again, the council has set in motion certain theological indicators for the future, even if the council itself did not enter into any doctrinal development in this area.

Thus the pastoral problem of what to do with the millions of Catholics involved in second marriages is still an open question. The past history of the Church in dealing with this problem is not all that clear or unambiguous. When people lived in small communities and where the average person never traveled more than ten miles from his village throughout his whole life, perhaps there was need for strict discipline in this area for the sake of scandal. This is no longer the case today and a whole new approach must be created. We are not here denying the possibility—perhaps probability—of sinful behavior on the part of one or both partners in the dissolution of the original marriage. We are speaking here of the people involved in second marriages *in fact,* whatever the sinfulness of past behavior. To insist on their "public sinner" status, first of all, is only to add to their already guilt-stricken position in society. Our society, no matter how liberal it may talk, condemns those who obtain divorces and fills these people with great anxiety and guilt—even when, perhaps, there was no guilt. The Church only adds to this guilt by the way in which she treats these people, and by her lack of counseling services precisely for people who are hurting so much. Moreover, in forbidding them the Eucharist—the very source of strength and faith—do we not make their position and condition that much more difficult since, in most cases, the dissolution of the second marriage is either impossible or would be actually ruinous for the spouses involved.

Priests, of course, must avoid true scandal in this area and, in order to avoid all semblance of permissiveness, must see to it that these couples are serious. Various criteria could be set up for such pastoral work but no hard and fast rules can be detailed since so much depends on the personal knowledge of the couple by the priest. Such criteria would include, at the very least: that the former marriage is truly dead with no possibility of reconciliation; that there is a reasonable assurance of the upright living and Christian strivings of the actual couple of the second marriage; that an honest attempt is made to give good Christian example to the children involved; that the spouses themselves desire, even long for, the holy sacraments of the Church; and that scandal is avoided, even if it means going to another parish for the reception of the Eucharist, etc. These are only suggestions but it would be wise to consult on a diocesan-wide basis with both the clergy and married people for more practical rules and pastoral guides.

What is asked of theologians above all is a more in-depth analysis of the constitutive elements of the sacrament of Christian marriage. Such a study cannot simply be theological or scriptural in nature, but must take into consideration historical and anthropological considerations. The study of marriage must be viewed certainly as an ideal (e.g. the Gospel injunctions of Jesus on marriage), but also as regards the practical possibilities of marriage here and now in this particular culture. It is only in this way that any healthy pastoral aid can be given to couples engaged in second marriages. For example, other cultures without exception uphold the ideal of a stable married state but do allow of exceptional cases where it would be deleterious both for the spouses as well as for the children to remain together. Divorce was and is always a possibility in such circumstances and this has not led to their being permissive in sexual matters. Only in the Roman Catholic Church is marriage regarded as absolutely indissoluble—a position which is becoming more and more difficult to sustain from a scientific point of view. In other words, the claim of the Catholic Church is dependent for its proof on a supernatural law and/or revelation which is unsupported by human experience, past or present, in other cultures of man. We must, in the Catholic Church, more honestly face the great abyss between the ideal of stable marriage, which is proposed in the theological manuals and the canon law codes, and the reality of marriage which people must in fact live day to day.

Even within the present context of law, the grounds for annulment can be and are being constantly enlarged. This is particularly true in the psychological area, where maturity of character is presupposed for a fully free decision to enter the interpersonal relationship which is marriage. When this has been found to be more or less lacking, can we say that a Christian marriage ever existed or, if there was a marriage, what the nature of that marriage can be, especially if we hold that personalistic love is the constitutive element of any marriage? When does that love become so weak—or so totally destroyed—that a true marriage no longer exists? For if the sacrament of Christian marriage is based on the analogy of Christ's love for the Church, when the relationship of the partners becomes actually destructive—for any number of reasons—can we really say that marriage from a Christian point of view any longer exists? And if we deny this, appealing to the "sacred bond" of marriage, what can this mean? It is not the "bond" which is sacred but the persons in the marriage. Moreover, what can we say of the Christian nature of the marriage of so many Christians who view faith as a simple formality or as a social necessity—"to be done" because "it is the thing to do"? Is marriage here based on baptism alone (the reason in present Catholic theology why consummated marriage between Christians cannot be dissolved) or should it be based on a mature faith? These are the questions which the theologian must ask for the future development of the sacrament of marriage.

Many times, under the present canon law, the invalidity of the first union cannot be proven in the external forum according to the present requisites. What is to be done in such cases, which are, in fact, the vast majority? Many parish priests simply resolve these cases in the internal forum without recourse to the complicated and usually unsuccessful procedures of the local tribunal. This is one way which pastors have used, but one, which for obvious reasons, is not ideal. More and more we must emphasize merciful internal solutions and a more pastoral approach in the external forum. We must emphasize—and perhaps set up special procedures and forums where couples can go— help for the couple to make, in conscience, the best decision. In such circumstances, the Church must more and more respect these conscientious decisions by couples by removing the present objectional laws ("public sinners") which serve only to create more guilt in these couples. This respect of conscience will have to be taken more seriously by the Church in dealing with these cases of decisions conscientiously arrived at by a particular couple. We must readjust our values, entrusting to God and the conscience of the couple the resolution of such marriages. Otherwise, we shall tend to exclude deserving couples from the Eucharist while "validly" married Catholics, who are far from being Christians in many other respects, have free access to the sacraments. As Father Orsy persuasively argues, in the matter of marriages whose invalidity cannot be demonstrated, the evidence of the parties immediately concerned should be accepted as sufficient; in cases where the local tribunal cannot act officially, there should be an official or quasi-official diocesan committee for counseling, in order to help the couples form their consciences as to the right path to take. It is precisely in this area where the much flaunted "religious freedom" text of Vatican II can be tested as to how seriously the Church herself takes it. There will be abuses (What institution does not have them?) but the greatest scandal of all would be to be so juridically intransigent (as in the present law) that the good cases as well as the bad ones are all judged indiscriminately and are all rejected. Responsibility here revolves directly on the couple who will be responsible before God for what the Church cannot humanly judge. There is no other pastoral way of dealing mercifully with these tragic cases of real life.

Part II

SPECIFIC SEXUAL
PROBLEMS TODAY

VI THE NEW SEXUAL MORALITY

The title of this chapter may seem somewhat ludicrous. Is there really a new sexual morality today? In a sense, yes. The attitudes of many people—particularly young people—seem to be changing with regard to sexual activity outside of marriage and cohabitation without marriage. Although this is nothing really "new," it is becoming a prevalent attitude among the young (and even among the not-so-young), so that a serious investigation of the reasons and justifications given for this new attitude is highly warranted by the religious community.

Our objective in this chapter is to subject to intense scrutiny the underlying justifications of this so-called new morality and to see whether or not it does change our traditional view of sex within marriage.

The younger generation prides itself on being more educated and more honest than any in history. There is nothing it fears or has hangups about, nothing it is unwilling to talk about or even experience. This is above all true of human relationships and sexuality. The "new morality," we are told, is more honest, healthy, and open than any in the past.

But already there are signs that one cannot discount the Ten Commandments with impunity, even if it is done honestly and with the best of intentions. Good intentions are not enough, as the drug addiction, broken marriages, and heightened anxiety among the young are beginning to reveal to anyone who deals with young people and marriage today.

Deep down, in spite of a better education, changes in the physical and biological environment, communications, etc., man remains morally about the same. In fact, within himself, man has changed very little (insofar as the record of history is open to us). He has the same rational as well as demonic (or, if you wish, irrational) elements within himself. My Lai should have disabused us all of the notion that our generation is the noblest of them all. We remain weak and sinful men within our own history.

Whatever else can be said of the older constraints and moral codes, they did in fact provide men with some sort of restraint on some of man's baser instincts and impulses. Hard as it is to admit, modern man is as beautiful and as vile as any of his predecessors of homo sapiens. The older codes provided a means of controlling and channeling man's natural selfishness, violence, jealousy, and possessiveness. They provided a structure in which there were clearly defined elements of guilt and praise.

Man, on his own, has a hard time deciding what the limits truly are. Is the only restraint on sexual relations, for instance, that you do not harm the other person, as many of the young claim? The older morality claimed a divine sanction for its defined limits ("Thou shalt not"), but a purely human ethic simply does not know the limits of this freedom or what actually does harm to the human person. So we ought to move very slowly in this area of sexual relations and be very careful before hastily joining a sexual freedom league. Why?

For the simple reason that the sexual in man is infected with the demonic, as is every other basic human instinct. Perhaps past Christian history went overboard (e.g., St. Augustine) in emphasizing the demonic within the sexual and did not stress enough the positive elements of growth, joy, and love. This may well be. But at least this tradition did not deny the base and vile within man. So the traditional restraints placed on the sexual did in fact remind man of a boundary beyond which he may not go without injury to himself and others. Whether this boundary was too narrowly conceived is another question. It is precisely this boundary to human sexual freedom which is denied by the young of today.

That the sexual is plagued by feelings of aggression, dependency, and possessiveness is simply denied by the young or is simply attributed to a puritanical hangup from another age. And yet, all around us is ample evidence that the sexual, unless correctly used and disciplined, leads to destructive consequences in human relationships.

Human freedom is never absolute. Man is free to the extent

that he recognizes the demonic within himself and tries to control and channel it to constructive ends. To deny that sexual aggression and exploitation exists in each one of us makes us incapable of dealing effectively with it. It is much like racial prejudice; if we deny its existence within us, this denial itself renders us incapable of effectively rooting it out.

The argument is usually given that traditional sexual morality has depended only on fear for its sanction. Now that the fears have been removed by the pill and penicillin for VD, the only moral criteria for sexual behavior, so the argument goes, are mutual consent and interest. College people are always spouting this moral line.

But is it so? Can simple moral criteria free man from the exploitative and possessive needs that are in each man? Hardly. And more and more psychological data is beginning to pile up to show that the traditional restraints in the Ten Commandments are not so much "horse feathers" after all.

Such studies as those of Rollo May in his outstanding work, *Love and Will,* and Victor Frankl in his *The Doctor and the Soul* have shown that modern society's preoccupation with eroticism is the direct flight from the meaning of love and death.

Rollo May shows clearly that the fulfillment of man resides in his ability to love others in total commitment and that only in this way can he face up to the great anxiety which is the mystery of human death. Seeking to escape this mystery and unwilling to give response to it by the commitment of love, modern man has tried to "blow his mind" in the sexual eroticism so prevalent in our society. The sexual separated from love is like any narcotic such as drugs and alcohol, that is, it is used as an escape and its results are the same: self-destruction manifested in manifold neuroses and even psychoses.

Frankl, in his books and lectures, has emphasized the same thing: man is made for meaning and he must give the sexual in his life meaning. This can be done only by the commitment of love. We have come full swing from Freud's day when many psychological difficulties were directly attributed to sexual frustration. Today this is no longer the case. Modern man suffers from sexual frustration—there is a glut of the erotic and the sexual—but from a lack of meaning to the sexual. This meaning can only be grasped when the sexual is integrated into human and committed love.

The "women's libbers" ought to be the first to recognize that the new sexual freedom has done very little to enhance the status of women. Some people feel that women's liberation demands that women be sexually liberated. (I am not speaking here of the whole of the women's liberation movement since in many political, social, economic, and ecclesial areas such liberation is badly needed. My basic argument here is only with those feminists who would identify "liberation" with open and free sex—a whole new and, given the experience of the American male, devastating ball game.) As women become more permissive, there is very little empirical evidence indeed that they are more esteemed as intellectuals or as social activists. They become glorified playmates, spouting liberation language but are as exploited sexually as they ever were.

In our culture, girls enter into a sexual relationship with a greater need for intimacy than boys. And should they complain that they are being sexually exploited, they are greeted with the charge that they are not "free," or that they suffer from sexual hangups from puritanical notions. These charges embarrass them into suppressing what they instictively know: they are sexually exploited and they will be the wounded "fall guys" when the relationship goes sour. It is they who will be psychologically maimed more than the male.

Moreover, the sexually permissive woman fulfills the exploitative masculine fantasy. She is equal in sexual matters but weaker and more vulnerable. She must pretend to enjoy all of her sexual contacts. This is the beginning of dishonesty because it simply is not so. The sexual fantasy of the American male has been fed by *Playboy* with the result that it is now easier for him to act out this stupidity on the "liberated" girl with devastating effects above all on her.

Moreover, she must deny her plight because otherwise she will be considered to be a "prude," an anathema considered worse than virginity itself. The result is that the "liberated woman" is more of a slave than her sister ever was who remained a virgin till marriage. This pretense of liberation becomes so bad that they do not even realize the true cause of the depression, frustration, and rage which they feel. They should feel liberated, but most of them are depressed. The answer is simple, but they dare not admit it: they are sexually exploited. Even many of our movies tend to emphasize this point with heroines who act out all the sexual fantasies of the "liberated" male only to find their lives boring, unfulfilled, and as empty as the males they jump into bed with. Whatever else they emphasize, these movies show how deeply unhappy female characters are when the sexual is not integrated with love.

At this late stage of the game, it is germane to point out that the sexual act is much more than a physical act that one can engage in at random or at will, such as one changes clothes. It is, of course, or can be, an act of love. But because of the demonic within man, it also is and can be, a means of gaining power, aggressively proving one's capabilities, flattering one's vanity, gaining reassurance, and relieving tension. The sexual in man is corrupted insofar as it is tainted with these not-so-beautiful instincts, and we close our eyes to the corruption of the sexual at our peril.

Take one example among many. Among young people, freedom of sexual encounter has as its greatest enemy, possessiveness. Faithfulness unto death is a hangup, a result of puritan and fear-filled upbringing, many young people would claim. It is assumed that the healthy person is free of possessiveness. Yet this is not at all true. Man's territoriality and acquisitiveness are biological "givens" which have not as yet been tempered by any form of social organization.

Konrad Lorentz in his book *On Aggression* describes the biological substratum of possessiveness which comes from a certain form of "territorial imperative." Each animal, including man, must have an area, some territory which he can call his own. The most disastrous consequences (war, cannibalism, fighting) follow when this basic biological law is disregarded or threatened.

Possessiveness is therefore a demand of biological life common to all animals. Man is different from the animals not in the sense that he can do away with this natural biological substratum (he cannot), but in the sense that he has reason and will to control and use it for his own good/bad ends.

Women above all (whether because of nature or upbringing is not important here—only the fact) are inclined to cling to those whom they love. Possessiveness can be very destructive but it is there nonetheless. The healthy person tries to control this instinct so that it does not lead to the hurting or stifling of those whom one loves. But it is there, rooted in man's bilogical drive for security, and it can be controlled, not denied.

Possessiveness is a primitive and biological way of demanding fidelity to commitment of one person to another. If possessiveness is denied, then what shall we substitute as a reminder of fidelity and trust?

The major goal of marriage is achievement of intimacy with another person in all dimensions of human existence. Intimacy depends upon trust and shared experience. It is very unlikely to develop between a couple who have serious reservations as to how long they will stay together. In other words, this intimacy is almost impossible (psychologically) unless there is a permanent commitment to each other in love. Otherwise the relationship is not worth the pain and agony demanded of two people trying to make a go of living and sharing together. People are unwilling to risk vulnerability, pain, and suffering, which are absolutely necessary for true intimacy and growth, without a definitive commitment to each other.

This commitment is called marriage. Consequently the "living together" and "trial marriages" of the young are not merely moral aberrations. More importantly, they are humanly ruinous. A good criterion of sexual morality is whether a particucalr activity promotes the truly human.

Couples who live together wish to believe that their relationship is more than a sexual convenience. To justify their sexual activity, they must convince themselves that they are on the way to true intimacy. But intimacy demands a commitment, or the pain just doesn't make it worthwhile. The result is that living together by young people without a commitment is already a mere pretense of intimacy. Their living together must either lead to marriage or it will be ruinous for the relationship. Freedom, ironically, demands commitment and this is what we call marriage.

The eminent psychotherapist Alexander Lowen has put it in the following way: "We cannot command our body to ignore the deepest truth it knows—that in opening itself to the possibility of pleasure, it stands exposed to the possibilty of pain. Furthermore, in the center of our being we are sharply aware that the greater the pleasure we enjoy today, the greater the pain we will suffer tomorrow if we lose the person who gives us the pleasure.

"The conscious mind may be willing to accept such a gamble, and desire can propel us into making it. But only if love is present will the body accept the gamble. For love is commitment, and with commitment, with faith that today's happiness will return tomorrow, the body opens to pleasure. Without commitment, with the clear knowledge that today's pleasure will be denied tomorrow, the body holds back. It remains tense and on guard, and cannot fully respond to another's touch. With love, however, with the feeling of total commitment that extends from the present to the future, the body willingly, eagerly surrenders itself. Thus love liberates our sexuality."

Trial marriages are bad psychology; therefore they are also bad morals.

There is one thing to be said for the young. They recognize very clearly that a life without values and order is a meaningless life. Yet, in the search for these values, our young people sometimes embark upon courses which are doomed to failure and frustration. Sexual freedom as practiced by some young people today is one of these disastrous courses.

Youth's attempt to find a substitution for the Ten Commandments has been a dismal failure from a psychological point of view. Nor does their dabbling in astrology, oriental meditation or mystical arts seem to be helping much. Neither can their pretense that the demonic within man and within the sexual does not exist help at all. In fact, such pretense is doomed beforehand to be shattered by reality.

Thus the traditional Judeo-Christian sexual code is far from being obsolete. In fact, after all the pretenses are over and the pragmatic codes are tested and found wanting, this code will again find a rejuvenation. Commitment and marriage are not simply moral demands; they are moral demands because they are human imperatives.

VII ABORTION

One of the greatest attacks on human life today is the almost universal clamor for "abortion on demand." The acceptance of abortion as a perfectly normal procedure for terminating pregnancy is becoming an accepted fact in American mores.

The question of abortion is highly complex and we have no desire to treat of it here in a popular book on sexuality and its problems today. However, this attack on human life cannot be passed over in silence for the simple reason that the witness of the Church to and for the human person would be put into deep question. This chapter will give some general observations as to the destructiveness of this practice and the courage necessary to uphold this value of human life.

Today we live in a society which is going to solve one of its major problems by abortion, further evidence of the increase of violence and disregard of human life. We seem to think we can solve problems by the gun, whether in Vietnam or in the ghettos, against whatever the local enemy happen to be—black, brown, Communist, Bircher, student, whatever the case may be. This society is going to solve its problems by violence and if anyone doubts it then let him simply look to the order of priority of spending in federal government and he will note how people live and enunciate their values in the way they spend their money. Show me how a people or a person spends his money and I will show you who he is. When we spend 75 percent of every tax dollar on war—past, present, and future—you have all the ingredients of a very sick society. So, as a continuation of this violence, we are going to solve another problem, but this time a self-inflicted violence, namely, the violence of abortion.

It is unfortunate that when we discuss abortion we seem to get all tied up in knots. We do not or cannot discuss this subject rationally and with discourse. We get terribly emotional and we begin to call people names: on the one side, directed against holding up progress—i.e., Catholics and others who think like them with regard to abortion—it is said that they are holding up progress or that they are trying to impose their private morality on the whole public; and on the other side against those who advocate a certain amount of reformation in such legislation, they are called "murderers" and "baby killers." At least let us be able to discuss the issues on matters of the issue itself and not simply on matters of emotionality. For this at least some knowledge of science, psychology, theology, and history is a prerequisite.

The first point to be made is that our tradition as Catholics is without ambiguity in this respect. It is the common experience of a basic truth which gives cohesion and substance so that without it neither the individual nor the institution can live. This truth, so realized, becomes the very substance of a man's being as well as of the community's.

It is at this fundamental point—that is, of the consciousness of the Church at her deepest level—that we can begin to approach the whole question of abortion in the mind of the Church. In two thousand years of the Church's tradition there is not so much as one small deviation from the consensus of the Catholic community that to kill any innocent human life, even the human life that is present incipiently but not distinctively within the womb, is a crime against God and man. From the very earliest days this moral consensus among the Catholic community is complete from any score. There were other moral problems where this consensus was not so clear from the beginning. For instance, the question of divorce and remarriage. For the first millennium the Church did in certain cases permit divorce and remarriage between married and Christian Catholic couples. We have these cases on record. There was an ambiguity in the Church's teaching both in the West and in the East for the first thousand years. The second thousand years has seen a different development to the point where we are now, but this does not negate the hesitancy on this moral teaching in the history of the Church. This poses a set of problems which, of course, is not my topic in this chapter.

In any case what I am trying to say is that in other moral problems, such as birth control and in divorce and remarriage, there were elements of ambiguity in various portions of Holy

Church, East and West, and consequently there was doubt on certain points as to the validity or nonvalidity of a certain teaching. This was not and is not now the case in the question of fetal life or life in the womb, however we wish to call it. Let us trace these salient points.

If there is anything in all of the Scriptures it is that all human life is sacred because it comes from God and may not be taken except for the gravest of reasons. In other words, the Scriptures always speak of life, birth, triumph over death, final and eschatological salvation given to us in Jesus the Saviour. As a matter of fact, when the Scriptures—but particularly the New Testament speak of death, it is only to show the omnipotence of God (in Christ) to raise from the dead—a work which completely escapes the power of man at any capacity. Therefore, the Scriptures in general have to do with openness to life and to salvation "for all human flesh."

The Old Testament is clear, even in the Book of Exodus (21:22-23), where the text calls for a fine imposed on anyone who brings about an accidental abortion in any woman. Of course, voluntary abortion was such a heinous act that it was not even mentioned in the Old Testament. The reason for this is that God's spirit, God's *ruah,* as the Old Testament puts it comes to inhabit man and man becomes a living being (*Gen* 2:7) because God's spirit comes to inhabit him. Man's dignity exists in the Bible because of his relationship with God, not with man. A man has an infinite dignity because he possesses God's *ruah,* God's spirit. He possesses this from God himself. So, in parenthesis, we immediately see a relationship throughout the Bible that is very clear, namely, that man holds his dignity in function of God, not of man. Once we say that man holds his dignity in function of other men or as the common cliches put it, "We have rights because the majority gives them to us" or "We have rights because the Constitution gives them to us," then we have inversed the biblical view. In Christian faith, man has dignity not because of a consitution or a law or because of a "majority." Our rights exist because we are God's creatures. I am God's life, and therefore I am a sacred being because my relationship is not man-to-man as the substance and origin of my dignity, but

God-to-man. Our society today has completely reversed this relationship in the question of abortion. That is to say that for convenience (let us be very honest with speaking of abortion, let us not bring out the tear jerkers of little nine-year-old girls being raped and of various cases of incest which are less than 5/10 of one percent. A large majority of abortions performed are on married women who don't want any more children), it is now man, on his own authority, who decides what life survives and what life dies. We have thus reached a perversion of the biblical view. In this new formulation, man's dignity and the dignity of human life resides no more on the relationship between God and man but upon the relationship between man and man and therefore one man, be it man or woman, can decide—for convenience or health or psychological equilibrium (as they say today) to terminate another *ruah,* another life. We have reversed the relationship and we have thus destroyed that which is taught in the sacred Scriptures. This is very serious consideration for those who have Christian faith.

Secondly, the New Testament teaching is very clear as well. There is no direct teaching on abortion in the Gospels, it is true, but there is the teaching of Jesus in the prophetical tradition, that is, Christ's kindness, love, going to meet and being sympathetic with the poor—understood in the broadest sense of the word as those who are without power, those who are destitute or dispossessed. The emphasis in the New Testament is the lordship of life over death, revealed to us in and through the resurrection of Jesus and in which all men have the power to participate by faith in the work of Jesus. Man is thus called to life, to bearing witness to the goodness of all life and all creation because it has been—at least in potency—transformed in the resurrection of Jesus over the power of sin and death which holds all men in bondage.

Since "church" is a continuation of that prophetical doing and teaching of Jesus in space and time, it is she who now has the mission to do what Jesus did: defend the poor and powerless against all forms of destruction and injustice. The Church becomes "church" radically when she defends the poor, when she defends the dispossessed, because the rich always have money and influence to defend themselve in laws or in legislatures, etc., etc., whereas the poor has no such resources. Thus it is that Jesus, in the prophetical tradition, takes up their cause, the cause of justice for those who cannot defend themselves. The Church becomes "church" nowhere better than when she defends those who cannot of their own accord defend themselves, and human life in the womb obviously cannot defend itself. The Church becomes a very beautiful defender of the rights and dignity of man when she says "no" to those who wish, on their own authority, to play God, to end such innocent life which only God, who has planted his *ruah,* his spirit, has the power to take away. The Church therefore is the continuation in space and time of the prophetical ministry of Jesus to the poor and dispossessed.

This is very serious. This mission runs throughout the Old and the New Testament, indeed, throughout the whole tradition of the Church. All the general and ecumenical councils from Nicea (325) to Vatican II (1965), all the popes from Peter down to Paul VI, all the provincial councils, all of them without exception call attention to this grave crime (it was called infanticide in the early Church). There is not a whimper of a doubt. The special heinousness of this crime was invariably punished in the canon law by special penalties ("excommunication") both in the Eastern and Western general provincial councils.

Therefore we must come to the conclusion that the Catholic experience, the experience that makes us to be a community, our specificity as community, is without a doubt at one of its profoundest levels, the dignity and the safeguarding of innocent human life in no matter what condition it is. The Christian Catholic is specified in this area by his dissenting and protesting against all those who would endanger innocent human life at any level.

On the one side, of course, we have those in our society who are going to solve all our problems by this little added element of violence. As they say, by abortion on demand, we can see "light at the end of the tunnel," with regard to solving our overpopulation or poverty problems. As a society, we will once again solve our social problems by violence, this time by turning the violence against ourselves. These people are absolutely inconsistent. On

the one hand, they protest all wars, as I do, whether it be in
Vietnam or the Near East. On the other hand they are willing to
turn violence, and indeed irresponsibility, upon themselves.

But, on the other hand there are the church people who say
that all abortion is wrong. I agree with them but the logical
conclusion of this is that all innocent life should be at our defense.
Where are these church people, for instance, in protesting capital
punishment? It has been shown time and time again that capital
punishment is not a deterrent to crime and yet we, particularly
Catholics, insist that capital punishment be kept on the books.

Where are the church people in protesting innocent life being
lost in Vietnam and the Near East? Where is their consistency
when speaking of the defense of the poor, the needy, the helpless;
the one million children, for instance, in California alone who
today suffer from malnutrition? Where are our petitions in the
back of the church, where are the bishops' statements in defense
of these people? For we must be logical with ourselves. If we
defend human life, we must defend it at all levels, whether in a
ghetto or with starving children or at a juvenile hall, or in Vietnam, or in a mother's womb. Either we defend all innocent
human life (because all human life represents the infinite dignity
of God, the *ruah*) or we defend none of it. To attack one
innocent human life is to attack all human life. This is very
serious argument, particularly among the young, against the
inconsistency of the Catholic community, and in this inconsistency we have lost the credibility of the young. They see us church
people as being intransigent when speaking of abortion but when
our attitudes against welfare are just as pagan as other people in
society: "welfare chislers," "we've got to crack down on those
spongers." We have all heard the whole thing time and time
again.

In a recent survey and in every survey I've ever found on the
question of solving problems by war or force, the Christians are
always more violent than the Jews and nonbelievers. And of all
the Christians, Catholics are the most violent of all the Christian
groups, outside of the Mormons. I think Catholics are running
neck-and-neck for bottom of the barrel insofar as groups who

advocate or solve problems by violence. This does not escape the scrutiny of the young.

It is at this point that we run into the greatest difficulty when speaking of abortion; that is, the *condition* of this innocent human life which is present in the womb. Some religious groups claim that such life is not "human" until the elapse of a certain period of time, and that until that time it is simply an appendage of the mother.

I do not wish to enter here into any extensive discussion concerning what a "person" is, or what "human" life is. I think that in our day it is safe to say that microbiology has clearly shown that from the very first moment of conception there exists a definite, distinct but by no means independent life. It has, in other words, if left to its own powers, all the potency to develop into an independent and self-sustaining entity. Geneticists would say that from conception itself it is a "genetic package" and time will only be that duration in which it will more fully become what it already is: a human person. At least if we understand "person" in the dynamic sense of the word as continuously becoming more itself in its self-reflectiveness and self-consciousness, which is a total process from conception to death itself. Every person alive is in the process of going from potency to act (to use scholastic terminology) in becoming even more itself. A demonstrable case, I think, can be made for seeing this process as a total whole and not separated or "begun" say at three or six months (as the medieval theologians thought).

In any case, the self-consciousness of the teaching of the Catholic Church is clear from the earliest days: innocent human life is one total whole. No one can take it upon himself to destroy or terminate his life whether at the beginning (abortion) during (murder) or at the end (euthanasia) of the human life process. There is a logical consistency in this universal Catholic experience which is marvelous.

Therefore, anyone in the Catholic community who does not agree with this moral consensus, with this double-millenary tradition, I think had beter revise his own mentality or perhaps look for another community. I say this advisedly. This is such a serious problem (innocent human life taken in abortion), and we attain the very heart of what it means to be part of a Catholic community, as distinguished from every other community, that a person who does not agree, attains one of the very rock foundations of the whole Catholic tradition that binds us together as an experience and as a community. The community does not exist without a history and an experience. Therefore, anyone who would radically disagree with this stand ought to realize how far he is from the Catholic experience. Any form of attacking innocent human life is entirely foreign to Catholic experience and it goes directly against everything we hold. I say this not to judge anyone because I know that there are Catholics who have literally been led astray by this type of mentality of the world seeping in, the false compassion that has been hammering at us in the mass propaganda media time and time again, so we must judge no one. But I do think that as a community there ought to be no doubt as to where we stand.

This moral problem ought to be clearly distinguished from the question of legality. There will be no agreement of views here among Catholics, as well it should be. This is so because of the question of application of morality to law, and when this happens there is a whole variety of differences among Catholics, and legitimately so. We must first clearly say that a law does not necessarily have to be totally in conformity with the moral order. The law exists to promote the temporal welfare and good of the people of a particular society. It is good law if what it commands is good, first of all, and if what it commands is obeyed by the vast majority of people in that society. We obey a law not because it is the law, but because what the law commands is good. Otherwise, we would have juridical positivism. We obey a law because what it commands is good. Just like we obey God not because it is his law but because what God commands is good. It is the good that we seek. Take, for example, the income tax. We all have gripes against income tax in general—I have mine with regard to military expenditures—but I think the essence of the law is quite sound; that is, equal distribution of burdens on a population to those most able to pay. This is clearly a question of social justice and, therefore, most of us pay our income tax because we see, begrudgingly sometimes, that what the law commands is good. We see this and we obey it.

The law in a civilized society is a teacher in the things that pertain to the commonweal. It shows people what is good for all, and its very binding power is not that it commands but that what it commands is good for the many in a society. Obedience to law then is a moral virtue and a moral obligation insofar as the law serves the good of men in a particular society. The good citizen obeys law not because he will otherwise be punished but because he knows the law to be good, in general and for many in society.

But law cannot be so much a teacher and guide as to be far from the moral consensus of a people on which it directly depends for its binding force. In other words, the law cannot enforce all good and must even sometimes regulate evil. Such was the case with Prohibition: there was no little moral consensus among the people and therefore the law became a mockery. It actually fostered disdain for the law. The same is becoming true with regard to the laws governing the use of marijuana. If its use becomes universal, then the law will have to be changed no matter if marijuana is good, bad, or indifferent. The moral consensus here has shifted and the lawmaker must take this into account.

So too with abortion. The moral consensus has changed and is rapidly changing, therefore the laws will be changed. I counsel all those for whom abortion is repugnant to simply not resist, because even if abortion laws remain on the books, they will be universally disobeyed, therefore bringing disdain on all law. Far better not to have any laws on the books governing abortion. In this way, we shall have had empirical evidence, one way or another, on how this shall have affected our civilization and the individual in our society. I think it will be a terrible way to learn this lesson, but I see no other way. Let us repeal all abortion laws, and see what happens. This logic is inherent in the present universal drive of the abortion nuts. Let them have their way and then let us carefully note and observe.

Is, therefore, a Catholic morally obliged to fight such legislation? Not necessarily. When he sees the good to be accomplished would be less than the evil; that is to say, in fighting such a law

(since it does not command us to have abortions), we must see
what the good and evil of such legislation would be. We are not
morally obliged to fight it if the evil will be greater than the good.
Certainly we have the right to fight politically, as citizens, individually and socially, but we have also the right, given the
circumstances, to acquiesce and I think that more and more we
shall have to do this. First of all, we are not forced to have
abortions. We must make a distinction in law: where the law
commands something and where a law *permits* something. Where
a law permits, you can have an abortion or not; no one is forcing
you. On the day they force us we can take up armed revolution.
Secondly, a law sometimes imposes something which poses its
own problem. The law, for instance, of conscription, says that a
Catholic young man must go to Vietnam even when he considers
the war in Vietnam to be an immoral war. We have great difficulties here. What we are doing is commanding someone to do
something against his conscience. Thus, there is a clear relationship to be made between these two forms of law.

A final moral objection against abortion is our almost total
ignorance of the long-term effects on individuals and on society
itself (human ecology). Ten years ago I wrote an article for
Catholic readers justifying (morally) the use of the oral contraceptive pills, but also warning of the possible dangers involved
because of our almost total lack of knowledge concerning the
delicate hormonal balance. This *caveat* was also moral because it
affected the person using the pill, but from another point of view.
My fears have since been amply justified. The same reasoning
must be applied to the present demands for easy, universal abortion. We simply do not know the possible grave consequences
for both individuals and society if and when such a policy comes
about. There is ample reason for moving very slowly in this area
because of our huge ignorance psychologically, socially, morally,
and even spiritually and economically! If there was ever a need
for the virtue of prudence, it would be in this delicate area of
abortion. But this is to be obscurantist and medieval or foisting
one particular morality on the whole populace—and all the rest
of the clichés of the abortion nuts who are going to solve the
world's problems (and women's liberation) by invading an area

we know pathetically little about! All the radicals in all the universities do not pose one greater danger to our country than these people.

In 1956, the government of Hungary—for purely economic reasons, since a Communist government has little regard for "morality"—permitted the easiest abortions in the world. Any woman, any time could obtain an abortion from any licensed physician in the country (if the physician refused, he could be prosecuted!). Last year, this law was abruptly repealed because of the great danger and damage which unlimited abortions had done to the *economy* of the country. Any physician today in Hungary who performs *any* abortion (except to save the physical life of the mother) is subject to the death penalty! This example ought to give the abortion nuts some food for thought, but it will not. There are few more dogmatic people than liberals who think they are right, because somehow they speak with the authority of God himself! Human experience, however, is not quite so dogmatic and it is our best teacher.

As a conclusion, let us simply say that our Catholic experience as a total community opposes all forms of abortion negatively, and protests and dissents from the spirit of the abortative society. It is here that we receive a real contextual realization of consciousness of being Catholic in our community, wherein we defend all forms of innocent human life. But this moral engagement as Catholics operating from our Catholic experience, must be distinguished clearly from legality where we as Catholics try to find the best solution, in context, to promote the peace and the common welfare. We can differ radically at this level and one solution will not necessarily be better than another.

VIII OVERPOPULATION

One need pay only scant attention to the mass media to know that in the United States one of the emphasized causes of pollution and future perdition is the so-called "population explosion." It has become a subject of such intense interest that many young people are refusing to have more than two children (when more are wanted, then, they claim, adoption is in order). Experts, such as Paul Ehrlich of Stanford University, predict great catastrophies in the near future unless stringent measures to curb population growth are taken soon. On the other hand, many Catholic moralists claim that there is no such problem today and to make such claims is to engage in scare tactics.

This chapter is an attempt to cut a mid-path between these two extreme positions. There is indeed a problem, and over the years, unless controlled, this problem will become greater. Therefore, it is important that Christians start thinking on this problem today so that something can begin to be done today, not tomorrow when the problem will even be greater.

It is not my intention here to go into any detail concerning the means used to control birth. I take it for granted that this teaching in the Protestant community is fully accepted and in the Catholic Church is in the state of flux. Theologically and religiously speaking, the question is today uninteresting since the basis for the responsible use of contraceptive means within a context of responsible marital love is almost unanimously accepted among Protestant and Catholic theologians, and it is not my objective here to cover that well-worked terrain at this time. Suffice it to say that what is about to be said with regard to overpopulation in both the overdeveloped and underdeveloped nations is nothing more than a pipe dream unless the use of artificial contraceptives in their various forms are fully accepted by all of the churches. For both intrinsic as well as extrinsic reasons, contraception is certainly one of the principal forms of birth stabilization for mankind for the indefinite future. Moreover, without it, there can be no hope for control and stabilization of world population. I take it as an empirical fact even though I have no intention of arguing the moral point at this time. The moral good of responsible contraception is evident on its face. The opposite would have to be shown in present circumstances.

Further, my intention is to address myself to the overpopulation presently obtaining between the so-called developed and underdeveloped countries themselves where, too, we are beginning to see the effects of too many people. We must here consider the qualitative as well as the quantitative effects of overpopulation. The former are not so obvious as the latter but they are present nonetheless, as anyone who travels in California knows when he sees acres and acres of good farmland torn up by the bulldozer for expanded homes, never (as food land and as natural beauty) to be replaced again. Indeed, most people are so insensitive to the problem that few Californians bothered to get excited when their governor, to justify the greed of the lumber industry, said that if you have seen one redwood tree, you have seen them all. Air pollution, water pollution, ear pollution, traffic congestion, overburdened public services—and many others— are seriously reducing the quality of life of even the most advanced industrial countries, and the population in these countries continues to increase (even with a modest 1½-2 percent *per annum*). The day most certainly will come when, so complexified will be the mode of life and so many demanding the better life, that government regulation of births will not be as farfetched as 1984. Indeed it might come precisely to this if population is permitted to go unchecked *voluntarily*. There are too many people; that is, in comparison with our present ability to organize even our own industrial society. There is a definite connection between our increase in population and the proliferation of our social problems, and Catholic thinkers have been absolutely unwilling to even think about this fact. Since men have a right not only to life but also to a more fully human life, even Catholics shall have to start thinking seriously about reducing our national population—at least until such time as we can learn to cope with the social and urban problems which we now have. This will come with great difficulty to the average Catholic who has been taught from time immemorial that large families are God's blessing and that to interfere with this "natural" process is one of the most serious sins man can commit. This whole mentality shall have to be radically changed in view of the present and future dangers of overpopulation on this planet. It will be a bitter pill for Catholics to swallow.

Our population has far outstripped our ability to solve the problems which such a growth has thrust upon us in the past 200 years. There is a definite limit on how many people can enjoy the good life and we have reached that point today. As a tentative conclusion, then, it would seem that we have a moral obligation to stabilize our present population until such time as we can reasonably solve our vast problems of urban blight and slums, even now occupied by the forty million Americans of the "other America." The tearing apart of land, uprooting of farmlands, communication problems, needed social services and institutions to serve the already harrassed population, the need for recreational sites—all seem to point in this direction. Indeed, it is probable that these demographic reasons of overpopulation in the overdeveloped nations would be moral reason enough for couples to limit sharply the size of their families today. In the past, the Church's stress on the quantity was justified as simply insuring the survival of the human race. One plague or natural disaster could wipe out three-quarters of the population. Today —outside of an all-out nuclear exchange—such a situation no longer obtains (indeed, just the opposite danger has now occurred), so that we are now before an entirely new situation. That is why the Church's teaching here must also change to meet this new situation. In this regard, the same moral principle applies—with regard to family limitation—domestically as well as internationally, since the demographic reason for family limitation is both qualitative as well as quantitative. In a highly complexified, technological, and overdeveloped nation such as the United States, this qualitative demographic reason for family limitation is of greatest importance. Few Catholic moral theologians have as yet addressed themselves to this momentous problem.

Overdevelopment is indeed a great problem for the future of mankind, but that is not what I wish to discuss here. The most urgent problem today is that of overpopulation or the relationship between the so-called underdeveloped nations and the industrialized nations, most from the North Atlantic. Moreover, by underdeveloped I do not mean culturally or morally but strictly economically, where the birth rate is so high that roughly three out of every four people there receive less than the recommended minimum daily calorie intake. Indeed, these people are hungrier now than they were several decades ago. In large parts of the world, the population is growing faster than the food supply. This is true mainly because of reduced death rates through the introduction of modern medical techniques, but sooner or later, unless birth rates are reduced drastically and correspondingly to the death rate, death rates will begin to rise as malnutrition overtakes medicine.

As is well known, the gap between the rich nations and the poor nations is growing each day. On the one hand, the computer-age technology is allowing the developed nations to forge ahead economically on a geometrical progression. On the other hand, capital shortages, lack of technical competence, and overgrowing population have prevented the "developing nations" (Asia, Latin America, Africa, the Arab states) from improving their economic condition to any significant degree. As a matter of fact, as their populations grow larger, their plights grow more desperate. Development aid in all forms from the rich to the poor nations has dropped from .9 percent of their GNP in 1960 to less than one-half of 1 percent in 1967, to .35 percent in 1969. Moreover, the aid is going further down, as witness 1971 when the United States Congress had before it the lowest foreign aid bill in history (.3 of 1 percent of the estimated 920 billion GNP). The volume and price of the exports of the developing nations continues to decline. The World Bank's interest is up from 6 to 6¼ percent on loans to the developing nations. The loans that they have already received from the rich nations are costing the developing nations some four billion in interest and principal payment. This figure must be subtracted from the global aid total of nine billion, which means, in effect, that the developing nations are receiving only five billion in aid—of all forms—each year.

The people in the "third world" who think that a solution to their poverty will come from the rich nations had better think again. Their greed is such that this aid will get smaller. These poor peoples of the world must depend on themselves, and one of their most potent weapons will have to be a reduction of their birth rate.

It is a truism at this late date to claim that in the world of today, the rich grow richer and the poor either remain poor or are actually becoming poorer. Seventeen percent of the world's people consume somewhat less than 80 percent of its goods, while the rest must subsist on what little remains. The United States consumes 50 percent of the world's wealth, and controls, directly or indirectly, 80 percent.

It is true that poor countries are poor partly because of their own lack of development and technical know-how, their background of colonialism and consequent retardation of industrial development (monoculture, etc.), and the manifold abuses of failure of distribution of the riches which are present in these countries. Not least of these causes remains their very high birth rate. All of this remains true and yet throughout the globe runs the revolutionary idea that a country or a people need not be poor or starving; that there is enough technical know-how to insure each man on the face of the earth a decent living and a comfortable existence. Poverty is not of itself a revolutionary factor; it is poverty which is realized as not inevitable that gives rise to revolutionary expectations throughout the third world of our day. This fact alone should impose a moral obligation on all men of good will, but particularly on Christians, to do all in their power to attempt to alleviate this miserable situation of the world's poor.

In his recent encyclical, *On the Development of Nations*, Paul VI reminded us that there must be a more reasonable distribution of the world's riches to the world's poor in the next twenty to thirty years. Somehow or other, means must be found to stem the flow of greater riches to the already rich, and greater misery to the already miserable. The nature of the present international system offers the poor nations nothing but despair. They are economically prostrate and, to date, the rich nations have offered them but two alternatives: either to attract new business and capital investment by massive preferential treatment, which is exploitation under a fancy name, or economic aid and loans with all of their concomitant political overtones. Both are simply modern forms of what both John XXIII and Paul VI referred to as "neo-colonialism" or manipulation of these poor countries economically and politically by the rich countries for their own ends.

Listen to the words of the World Bank, which speaks for the rich countries: "The continued swift growth of the industrial countries as well as some replenishment of their stocks of primary materials, which will depend in part on the state of international tension, may well increase their demand for imports from the developing countries at a higher rate than last year." In other words, the developing (poor) nations are dependent upon more Vietnams in order to profit economically. The irony is not missed by the poor nations, who know that these wars are in fact fought by the rich nations *in the very nations of the poor* (Dominican Republic, Vietnam, Korea, Guatemala, Cuba) and will continue to be so for the indefinite future. In other words, the poor countries will participate economically in their own bloodletting. There must be some other avenue out of the agony of the poor nations. There must be some other way than the totalitarianism of the Marxists or the bombs of the Americans.

This is not all; economists and demographers well know that the gap is widening. A bishop from one of these poor countries recently told me: "My people live not only in poverty but in permanent misery." This poverty brings about all types of human sufferings. The first is the nagging, painful hunger in the pit of the stomach which can never be satiated, day or night. In 1966 alone, some twenty-five million people (among these, millions of innocent children) literally starved to death on this globe. Poverty brings diseases that cannot be cured, because there are no medical facilities. Illiteracy abounds in these lands, where the great majority can neither read nor write. This poverty breeds slums that make Harlem look good by contrast, whether we call them slums, bidonvilles, or favelas. This poverty breeds crime and vice on a scale that would stagger any civilized human being. Poverty in these countries means that most people will die before they reach the age of thirty-eight and that death will be a sweet release.

The worldly paradox comes into play when we realize that for the first time in history we have the technical know-how to wipe out all poverty from the face of the earth. What is lacking is not the resources or the money to do so, but the will to do so on the part of the wealthy peoples of the earth. This is a fact. Last year the Congress of the United States grudgingly gave 1.8 billion dollars to strengthen the weak economies of the poor nations. This was only after earnest pleas from the president and many brutal arguments on both floors of Congress. The eighty-billion-dollar military budget to be used for destruction, death, and if necessary, murderous nuclear intent, was approved in a matter of minutes, with no debate. American Christians must seem a strange breed of Christians when year in and year out they countenance such mockery and hypocrisy on the part of their representatives. We give double that for dog and cat food.

What must be categorically denied then is the whole philosophical and theologial basis on which both the domestic and foreign policy of the United States is founded. It is founded on keeping the majority of mankind poor while the few rich nations (above all, the United States), can retain their privileged position of wealth and power all over the world. History shows that the rich seldom give up power (economic or military) without a violent revolution, and since such revolutions will mean a deterioration of the unique economic and military power of the United States, all "subversions," "wars of national liberation," must be opposed all over the (poor) world.

The real revolution alive in the world today is not "Communism vs. Free World" or "freedom vs. slavery"; this is just so much political as well as moral rubbish to alleviate the consciences (most "Christians") of the few rich (18 percent of the world) who possess the great majority of the world's wealth (about 80 percent). These rich nations know that if they were to give up their privileged positions (e.g. international trade, stabilization of prime products from the poor, monopolistic interests financed by American dollars with the cooperation of corrupt local oligarchies) then they would have to share wealth with the mass of humanity. This would run contrary to the present policies of the rich nations, above all that of the United States. That is what seventeen Catholic bishops from the underdeveloped "third" world were talking about in their letter on revolution to the poor countries of the world:

> The people of the third world form the proletariat of today's humanity, exploited by the great nations and menaced in their very existence by those who alone claim the right (because they are stronger) to be the judge and the policemen of the people who are poorer.

There can be no doubt that these bishops meant the United States, particularly in its relationship to Vietnam and the Dominican Republic. These churchmen made the explicit point that the Church should endeavor to end all of its ties to that system which is above all "the international imperialism of money." In the face of this attitude of the rich and powerful nations, the poor take matters into their own hands, even if it is by violent revolution against this international system of capitalism and money which keeps them poor. "It is time that the poor people (of the world), sustained and led by their legitimate governments, efficaciously defend their right to life." In order to accomplish this, these bishops forthrightly claim that:

the Church does not condemn every revolution;

the Church wishes those revolutions which lead to justice;

the Church knows that, often, it is the rich and not the poor who are responsible for class warfare. Unless this can be changed peacefully, it will be changed violently, and with moral justification on the part of the poor.

The bishops are quite blunt in their language but they give the true cause of revolution all over the globe. Communism does not and cannot create these conditions; it can only make use of them for its own goals. Marxism is a definite even if brutal solution to this tragic problem of poverty. The Americans, however, are looked upon *universally* as the enemy of the poor, and they have the proof at hand: the Americans are willing to spend fifty billion dollars a year to destroy this revolution of the poor in Vietnam, and although they mouth all the right words about poverty in the world, they really don't believe it since they allocate a miserable two billion dollars for the poor of the world— and this mostly in loans! The poor must realize on what side the Americans will fight in a true revolution of rich and poor and that is why these same bishops bluntly told their flocks:

> The poor . . . know by experience that *they must count only on themselves and on their own forces rather than on aid from the rich* . . . It would be an illusion to passively expect a free conversion of all those whom our father Abraham told us about: 'They will not listen even if one from the dead speaks to them' (*Lk* 15:31). It is first of all the job of the poor . . . to accomplish their own promotion themselves. (Italics mine)

The bishops might well have added that their poor people may well expect green berets, napalm, and other "military advisers" lined up against them and with the established oligarchies. This is true of practically any country in Latin America.

The bishops are saying nothing more than that rather revolutionary encyclical of Pope VI, *On the Development of Nations*.

The principles of redistribution of wealth, says the Pope, ought to be such that it guarantees to each individual nation, *as a right*, in the world community sufficient resources to permit its citizens to live a decent, human, economic, and social existence; in its turn, the recipient nation would contribute according to its own means and resources. The terms of exchange would be submitted to objective and strict terms of social justice in conformity with the well-known adage of social justice: to each according to his needs and from each according to his abilities. This principle of moderate socialism runs throughout the encyclical (pars. 1, 6, 15, 17, 20, 22, 26, 28, 34, 39, 47, 65, 79).

This, of course, is diametrically opposed to the atomistic and capitalistic system which presently rules and does violence to the international commercial system (par. 26). The distress in the present economic and social sphere on an international plane is not dependent on any particular individual or group of individuals, but on a whole system of capitalism which runs its own course with its own laws and which can be cured only at the root cause: personalizing that which has been brutally and inhumanly depersonalized in this system. The distress proceeds from a profoundly dislocated social and economic structure on the international scene and as such has an inhuman effect on the human person—particularly the poor since it reduces men and nations to a means for economic progress and gain and profit motive. Since capitalism is based squarely on the profit motive, it cannot be made into any kind of principle for the solution of the world's poor. On the contrary, it is directly inimical to them above all. We shall have to find more equitable and efficacious means to promote this international social justice *founded directly on the principle of the solidarity of the human family and on no other* (cf pars. 3, 5, 44, 48). The Pope is speaking then, not of a question of "foreign aid" or "charity" (even if they are needed as a stop-gap measure for the present), but of a matter of strict social justice. Otherwise, it will become simply impossible to stop—let alone alleviate—the slide of the poor nations into further degradation. This calls for an international taxation on actual income to be thereby redistributed internationally as regard to actual need (par. 47).

To all of this of course, we must also recognize that a growing population in both the overdevelped and underdeveloped countries is bound to increase the mounting tensions between them. Each additional American—indeed, each additional person born in the developed nations of the world—owing to the high standard of living, will consume a disproportionate share of the world's goods. Indeed, given the imbalance and totally unjust terms of world trade, this will come at the expense of the already poor of the developing nations. And these goods will be consumed at a time when these resources are getting scarcer and scarcer. This is true of even the most basic resource of them all—food.

In a much overlooked bulletin released jointly by the Departments of State and Agriculture last year, it is stated that by 1984 no amount of aid from the food-surplus countries, even if we turned loose our full productive capacity, would be able. if present trends continue, to prevent massive famine in the have-not nations. The spiral mentioned earlier will then have reached international catastrophe unless some drastic steps on population stabilization and economic development can take place.

In light of these imminent events, it is positively immoral for the Catholic Church to withhold approval of birth control techniques even if for no other reason than avoiding the lesser of two evils (the starvation of millions of human beings). Surely such an historical circumstance must indicate to the Church, on an objective level, that the historical situation of mankind has radically changed, and that, therefore, her traditional teaching on birth control must now radically change. Such a change is not a giving in to the "spirit of the world" or the selfishness and hedonism of modern man but rather an objective and compassionate response to the absolute needs of the men of our day.

In these parts of the world where population growth is so great in proportion to available resources, it does not take much knowledge to recognize that the relatively high birth rates should be lowered as soon as possible; yet as the history of family regulation in the industrialized West suggests, it may be impossible to achieve any substantial, lasting gains in this regard until more ample economic opportunities become available and are recognized as in some way attainable by the majority. In other words, it appears that the observed reluctance of many couples in economically underdeveloped societies to limit their family size is not owing primarily to ignorance or indifference to hunger, sickness, and suffering, but indicates that their interrelated systems of social organization and motivation, traditionally geared to unrestricted procreation, have not yet been affected sufficiently by change to make family planning meaningful to most individuals. Therefore, these societies seem to be overpopulated not because of ignorance but because of lack of motivation for doing so—as indeed obtains in the developed nations. Therefore, once again, a vicious circle in underdevelopment, overpopulation which leads to further poverty and underdevelopment. It is only economic development—and not the spread of contraceptive information and devices—which will change the attitudes and motivations of the poor of the world. It is, therefore, imperative that as churchmen we see the moral connotations of *both* technical aid and population control. Indeed, there is great danger in stressing one (population control) without the other, for the poor will see this as a means of neo-colonialism or of downright genocide. It must be galling indeed to the poor in Southeast Asia or Latin America to see Americans setting up birth control clinics while these same Americans pay them a starvation wage for their coffee or sugar on the international market. We have no moral right to approach the poor of the world with birth control information without a corresponding effort at technical and economic aid in much greater quantity than in the past. Indeed, this will be seen by the poor as positively obscene on the part of the complacent and greedy rich. This economic aid to the world's poor cannot be given in any sufficient degree as long as their is any great increase in the populations of the developed nations who each demand vast quantities of the already scarce resources of the world. The United States must simply decrease its own population explosion since the United States and other advanced countries simply do not exist in an economic vacuum. We live in luxury in a world the majority of whose people live in want and destitution.

Many Americans find it hard to understand how the backward peoples of the world can accuse us of "imperialism." But modern imperialism—as Pope Paul VI has shown in his encyclical *The Progress of Nations*—does not require the possession of colonies. It merely requires the existence of more and more Americans living well in a world that is starving.

The moral question—if my economics and demography are correct—for the Catholic Christian ought to be quite evident. If growing numbers of Americans actually do deprive many of the world's people of the necessary resources needed for human existence, then Americans have a moral obligation not to increase their population at the present time. This is a moral obligation incumbent upon the nation as a whole and upon individual

American couples in particular. If having more than three children per couple, for example, will increase the population—with all of the consequences for the international community already mentioned—then each couple in the United States as well as in the rest of the developed countries, has a moral obligation of having no more than three children per family. This moral obligation seems rather clear on its face.

Moral theologians have always claimed intrinsic as well as extrinsic reasons for limiting the size of families. That is, the reasons were intrinsic insofar as these relate to the condition (economic, physiological, psychological, etc.) of the couple themselves or the children already born. The reasons are extrinsic when they relate to conditions outside the immediate family. Thus demographic reasons of either absolute (the whole globe) or relative (a particular nation) overpopulation have been seen by moral theologians as an extrinsic reason for family limitation. This reason can be considered both regionally (for instance, the situation in the overdeveloped countries, such as obtains in the United States) or on an international basis. Given the active interaction of the economy of development, plus the growing scarcity of available goods in proportion to the number of people, it can be seen that such an obligation falls directly on the couples of the developed nations. It is they who have the motivation and the knowledge necessary for such a step—so as to be able to share more with the developing nations, in whose turn, proper motivation for family limitation will increase in proportion to their growing development. A couple has no right to bring many children (at least more than is necessary to stabilize the present population growth at present levels) into the world when they know that such additional mouths will consume great quantities of goods and services—owing to our high standard of living—at the cost of depriving or even retarding the economic growth of countless children throughout the mostly poor world which comprises over two-thirds of the population of the globe. The moral obligation here seems to be clear.

It must also be clear that this is not the total situation or solution since it is evident that this trend can be ambiguous;—that is, smaller families can simply proceed to consume ever greater amounts of goods. Thus the obscenity of American children with electric toothbrushes while children in Latin America go without a cup of cold milk. This same situation is above all present on our domestic scene as well. In 1967 personal incomes of Americans increased over 16 billion dollars while the Negro community simply became poorer than before. There was, and, for the foreseeable future, there is no effort to redirect these funds to the poor even domestically.

What is morally true of nations can also be true of individual couples. Having less children, their efforts, talent, and resources must be drastically increased on behalf of the poor peoples of the world. For the Christian, the moral obligation here is very clear. Birth regulation to be moral must be responsible, and it is an act of the greatest irresponsibility to decrease the number of children in one's family so as to become ever more selfish and materialistic. We are released from one responsibility—many children—so as to be more generous and responsible for the other children of God in the world. It is not just the individual who has a right to life, but the whole of the human family as well. It is destructive of brotherhood for one small group to have many children at the expense of other brothers who are at the banquet of life. We are responsible not only for our flesh and blood but for all men; we are either our brother's keeper or we shall return to the barbarism of the survival of the fittest, or richest. We have no alternative to brotherhood.

IX WOMEN'S LIBERATION AND THE GOSPEL

As Pope John XXIII pointed out in his encyclical Peace on Earth, *one of the most revolutionary aspects of our times is the liberation of women. At this point in history, we do not know what directions this new start in human history will take. What we do know is that the essential drift of this movement is in profound harmony with the Gospels themselves and that it is none other than Jesus himself who relates always to women as persons, never as sexual objects.*

In this chapter we will endeavor to illustrate this basic point, arguing from the Gospels and the example of Jesus himself. This method, of course, does not begin to solve the many concrete problems of woman's role in history today, but it will give us a spirit and a foundation to seriously carry through this revolution of modern times.

It is only a fool of a man who would attempt to speak with authority on the subject of women's liberation today; that is, to try to explain to women who women are today. Moreover, for too long priests and bishops have attempted to do this in common teaching in classrooms and in pulpits. The Church itself, completely dominated by males, has time and again attempted to tell women what and how to think of themselves, mostly within cultural patterns which have always emphasized the domination of females by males.

It is, therefore, supremely important, if we are to understand anything of what is happening today in the area of women's liberation, to see that we as a society are dominated by a double history; both aspects have tended to consider women as inferior beings. The first is that of secular history where women from recorded history have been relegated to an inferior position in society by polygamy, sexual expolitation, easy divorce only for men, being treated as nonpersons, and educationally neglected in the extreme. A woman's role was considered to be no more or no less than what the Germans called *Kirche, Kuche, Kindern* (church, cooking, children); in these things the totality of her life was summed up. The second aspect of our culture comes from our religious history, which has also excluded women from any productive role by a male priesthood and hierarchy.

First, let us discuss some aspects of secular history. We have no intention of covering the vast field of the political exploitation of women. Suffice it to say that it was only in 1922, even in the United States, that women received the right to vote. We as a society have not as yet begun to realize the revolutionary implications and possibilities of this crucial fact. In many places of the world, this simple political reality is not yet a fact, and there women are still back in the dark ages with regard to realizing their own potentials. We shall restrict our remarks, however, to the United States where our experience is greatest.

While it remains true that women in this country exercise the vote, it is not at all certain whether they have realized the implications of this political reality. Women in fact outnumber men, 52 to 48 percent, and it is hard to imagine a nation fighting a war, children going hungry, or a distorted sense of priorities being allowed to exist in a country where 52 percent of the votes were against it. What in fact has happened is that the women of the United States have allowed themselves to be cowed by men and their distorted ideals and policy objectives which have brought us to the brink of catastrophe. In a recent *Newsweek* survey concerning the Hatfield-McGovern Amendment (to remove all United States military personnel of whatever kind from Southeast Asia by the end of 1971), some 50 percent of the males queried agreed with this proposition whereas some 63 percent (two-thirds) of the females queried, agreed with the proposition!

It is evident that women have used very little of their power toward constructive ends. It is conservatively estimated that women own about 60 percent of all the corporate wealth of the country. If money is supposed to speak and have power, then women have truly failed to use the power which they already have for peace and antipollution goals.

Another aspect of history is the evident fact that women have been sexually exploited through the ages. This is of course evident today in the form of the Playboy philosophy so rampant today in the United States. Women are bunnies and playmates for men and, therefore, objectives (for commercial gain) of male lust. This is evident all the way from the form of clothing women wear to the way in which advertisements sell everything from cars to medicine by the image of the sexy chick. The exploitation resides in this, namely, that in each case, women are wanted for their beautiful bodies and feminine allurements but in fact are treated as objects and never as persons.

To treat another as a person is to respect the totality of that person which includes the heart, the mind, the desires, the body, and the psychology of that person. To separate the sexual-genital from this totality is to degrade the person to the level of an object. Yet, to be sexually exploited also includes relegating women simply to the procreative function, as has been so common in the Christian West. St. Thomas Aquinas once said that, all things being equal, it would be better for a man to relate to another man rather than a woman. St. Augustine even advised older couples who were incapable of having children, to refrain from sexual intercourse since conception could no longer take place.

The modern emphasis on developing woman as a total person, socially, politically, intellectually, etc., is a definite step forward. This is facilitated today by the fact women live so much longer than in past history. They are around not only longer than men (73 years is the average life span for women in the United States, but more importantly, they are around some 35 years *after* their last child leaves home to make it on his own. This leaves a great amount of time for boredom or for active expansion and development of their persons. But is could also open up vast possibilities for education (if only the colleges and universities would open up to this great dimension of the future) and professional contribution to the world. It is not uncommon for women to take to alcohol, leave home, divorce, have mental breakdowns of varying degrees, or simply mentally and psychologically die during these critical but mature years of human growth. This is the fault of both society and of women themselves who have not prepared themselves for this period of their lives.

There is, of course, another obstacle to the full personalization of women in history which must be faced, namely, the obstacles which come from religious history. To a large degree, religions have tended to subjugate women, assuming the cultural mores of time and place rather than the implications for personhood contained in religion itself. This is above all true of the religious history of Christianity.

There can be little doubt that the essential core of Christ's teaching in the New Testament (which we shall see later in more detail) in no way discriminates against women. Indeed, they are treated and taught by Christ with dignity and respect for their persons. However, when Christianity became the religion in many places, instead of carrying out the radical reforms implicit in the Christian religion vis-a-vis women, Christianity simply adopted the cultural *mores* (male domination) of the Roman, Greek, and Near Eastern empires which further came to influence the proper structures of Church organization which also became male dominated.

We can see this today. Canon 16 of the official Code of Canon Law of the Catholic Church still places women—as to juridical effects—with children and idiots. Another canon (not practiced today but still on the books) encourages pastors to separate the men on one side of the church from women and children on the other! Even today, a woman reader of the Scriptures at Mass or other liturgical functions is frowned on by church authority. Moreover, every woman is forbidden to read from *within the sanctuary,* a residue of the Old Testament where women were forbidden access to the interior portion of the temple because they were "unclean," that is, they suffered from a menstrual flow of blood.

It is also a well-known fact that women cannot be ordained to the priesthood or be elected bishops or popes. This question, of course, was never seriously posed as long as it seemed "natural" that only men have access to these offices in a male-dominated culture. Today, this has radically changed and we are now before a whole new historical situation where the practice of the

Church must also change. There is absolutely no dogmatic or scriptual reason why a baptized female believer cannot be ordained or elected bishop or pope.

For years, the argument against this was that Christ only chose men as his apostles. Besides not being entirely accurate (the first apostle to the pagans was a woman, namely, the Samaritan woman), Christ could not have done otherwise, given the actual historical and cultural situation of the time. This has now radically changed and so must the discipline of the Church in this regard—or at least consider the *possibility* of a change if pastoral needs so warrants it. Women simply cannot be excluded from the priesthood on any dogmatic or scriptural considerations.

We can also see this exclusion of women from vital areas of the Church's life. We saw this recently at Vatican II where there were some 3,500 men legislating for over 50 percent of women (of their constituencies) while there were only three rather feeble female "observers" at the council itself. The Birth Control Commission established by John XXIII and continued by Paul VI had only three married women on it, in spite of the evident fact that birth control vitally affects *both* men and women.

Moreover, religious orders of women are also dominated almost completely by males. They are subject to the local bishop who is a male; they must have a "Cardinal Protector" in Rome, once again the sign of paternalism by men over women who need "protection." They must submit rules of their life (and practically all changes) to the Congregation of Religious which is almost all male dominated. It is now evident to all how archaic this whole set-up is for religious women totally subjugated to men. Today such a situation is totally anachronistic, where women have long since left this condition of oppression and dependency on men for their secular and religious lives.

This brings us to the point we made earlier. Jesus never oppressed women in any way—as was the usage of both the Judaism and rabbis of his day and age. Women were not to be seen in public or taught in any way, and they were to occupy a totally secondary position in religion and its practice. They were not even to be spoken to by any self-esteeming rabbi who valued his public reputation. Not so the evident example of Jesus which the New Testament gives us. Jesus spoke to women in private and in public; he taught them along with the men; he respected and honored their persons, not simply as sexual objects (wives, mothers, prostitutes) but as children of God called to love and salvation with men and on a par with men.

We can see this in many Gospel narratives. When at the home of Martha and Mary, Jesus taught Mary who sat and listened to him. Martha did not think (along with other good Jews of the time) that this was the place for a woman and she complained to Christ that Mary should do what a woman is supposed to do: take care of the house and do the cooking: "Martha, Martha, you are anxious about many things. Mary has chosen the better part and it will not be taken from her," was Christ's response to the complaint. This was astounding since most rabbis of Christ's day thought that it would be better to burn the *Torah* than to teach it to a woman. A woman, in Christ's view, has as much right as a man to listen and learn the Word of God. A woman cannot be reduced to simply housekeeping chores.

Jesus loved women (which is the only real way to treat any person as a person) and the Gospel of John says very simply that "Jesus loved Martha and Mary." Many of Christ's miracles were performed at the instigation of faith of women in the gospels. This is abundantly clear in the example of the Syrophoenician woman (Mark 7:26). The woman persists in her faith in spite of the fact that Jesus almost goes out of his way to insult her in order to test her faith: "It is not right to take the children's bread and throw it to the dogs." Any man would have been insulted at this reference and turned away in disgust. Not so the woman: "Yes, Lord, yet even the dogs under the table eat the children's crumbs." Christ is overcome by the faith of a woman! He exclaims in utter admiration at her faith: "Oh, woman, great is your faith!" (Matt 15:28). Only two places in all of the Gospels does Christ praise the great faith of two persons: a Roman centurian and a pagan woman—both the despised people of the time.

Moreover, the first apostles of the "good news," that is, the resurrection, were women and this is not by chance. Each of the

Gospels goes out of its way to stress the fact that those who were faithful to Christ to the very end (women) were rewarded for their fidelity by being the first to hear and announce the good news of resurrection of Christ. It was women and not men who were, once again, the first apostles to announce this good news, particularly emphasized by the fact that in Jewish law, the testimony of women was without value.

The most evident example of Christ's respect for the person of women was his dealings with the prostitutes and women of ill repute—which no self-respecting rabbi would ever even consider. Christ judged each person on his own merits, by his own repentance and faith, irrespective of who they were: pagans, Jews, soldiers, tax collectors, prostitutes, leaders, men, and women.

Christ never had a harsh word for any of these women or men. He allows them to touch him as was the case of the prostitute who washed his feet and dried them with her hair (Luke 7:36). The pharisee (Simon) who invited him was aghast at this but Christ responds simply, speaking directly to the woman (unhead of for a rabbi to do): "Your faith has saved you; go in peace." The woman was a lowly sex object in the eyes of all (she was a prostitute) but in Christ's eyes, she was simply a person, a child of God, who by her faith came to love much and therefore be saved.

The example of the woman taken in adultery is still another case in point about Christ's unprejudiced views (John 8:1-11). The pharisees bring a woman caught in the act of adultery to Christ for judgment (notice: it is only the woman who is brought and not the man!). They ask Christ to decide whether to obey the law of Moses (stone her) or to kill her in the Roman manner by crucifixion, etc. Roman law had forbidden the exercise of Jewish sacral law in civil matters and the punishment of stoning. In either case, Christ would compromise himself; either with the Roman authorities or with the people among whom he had the great reputation for kindness and forgiveness. Christ simply says that the one without sin ought to throw the first stone— which solved the problem immediately, for all men are sinners, starting with the eldest who had more years to commit more sins.

Christ then exercises the greatest compassion and no condemnation: "Neither will I condemn you; go and sin no more." Christ's attitude in the face of the most degraded people of the times in which he lived was one of only the greatest respect for the person of the sinner.

There are two other examples where Christ's attitude and respect of women lead to his rejecting the male-prejudiced view of women. The first was the case of the woman who suffered from a flow of blood (some women, at certain times of the month, were considered to be ritually unclean because of the flow of blood (the sign of life). During menstruation, everything which they touched also became unclean, so they were forbidden to touch anything during this period.

One can begin to understand with what fear and trepidation the woman with the flow of blood approached Jesus and *dared* to touch him, hoping for a cure. Christ turns and asks who had touched him. The apostles understood this in a physical sense saying that in the crowd, all manner of people were touching him. But Christ evidently means a touch of *faith and love*. The woman, fearing judgment confesses what she had done. Christ simply rejects the law that such women were "impure" and praises her for her faith. Once again, Christ is a respecter of persons, irrespective of sex and condition as well as of ritual law. It is the heart of the person that matters. The example here, once again, is the *woman* of faith, the despised and unclean woman who comes to faith and is, therefore, healed and praised.

The final example is that of the woman in the crowd who, after hearing Christ teach the people (which was itself instructive, since he also taught *women* publicly), praises him by saying in an almost reductive sense: "Blessed is the womb that bore you and the breasts that you sucked" (Luke 11:27). We have here the perfect example of what a woman is, namely a purely sexual object who bears babies, takes care of them, and makes love to men. It is the perfect embodiment of the male-dominated society where woman occupied this restrained area of human existence. Christ responds in a most contradictory way: "Blessed rather are those who hear the word of God and keep it." Christ corrects this view of women since she, along with the male, is

called upon to listen, understand, and accept God's word. By one
stroke, Christ simply says that woman is much more than simply
a sexual object. She is a child of God, called to eternal life on a
par with males, and must respond with freedom, intelligence,
and love.

Christ's teaching on marriage is also instructive with regard
to the equality of woman. In Jewish law, only the man could
obtain a divorce and he could do it for the most frivolous of
reasons (even if he did not like his wife's cooking) and send her
back to her parents. Woman (the wife) was nothing more than
the property of the husband who could dispose of his property
in any way that he saw fit. Christ completely destroyed this male
myth and pride by saying that marriage is built on love and
equality. He refers to the text in Genesis (Matt 5:31-32; Luke
16:18; Mark 10:11-12) where God made man and woman
one by joining them forever as one flesh. Divorce was therefore
clearly out of the question for either man or woman because of
God's holy law from the beginning. Man could no longer treat
his wife as a thing or property to be disposed of as he saw fit;
she was "flesh of his flesh and bone of his bone," that is, she is
the same nature, dignity of person as he. Polygamy is out, divorce
is out because of the equality of the couple and the dignity of
woman.

This attitude of Christ was so astounding and unheard of in
the ancient world that even the apostles were nonplussed: "If
this is so, then it is better not to marry." Jesus answers that his
teaching on marriage is hard but that with God's help it can be
done: "Not all men can receive this precept, but only those to
whom it is given" Matt. 19:11). To respect the persons of others
by love requires the abiding grace of God, which must also be
applied today in our search for safeguarding and promoting the
dignity and personhood of women.

One could cite other examples from the Gospels but it is
enough for our purpose to have brought out these few examples.
The conclusion from all this ought to be quite clear to us. Jesus
did not buckle under to the male prejudice and domination of
his society. He rejected it out of hand in both his practice and
in his teachings. Woman has the same dignity, call, and respect

as man and, in this sense, there is no such thing as an inferior position of woman before God. They are equal to men in their own human dignity as well as intellectually. Their intelligence should and must be developed along with that of men. He never looked at them as pure sexual objects (wife-mother-prostitute) but rather as persons with equal dignity to be loved and respected in their own right.

The Gospels are clear on this attitude and teaching of Jesus. Unfortunately, the Church, developed in male-dominated societies and her own structures in history, became dominated by this male mentality and arrogance. The Gospel contradicts this mentality which is in no way "natural" or "willed by God." It can change, and if pastoral reasons warrant it, it ought to change. The Gospel, of course, will not solve all the problems of woman's dignity which have taken thousands of years to solidify and strengthen. But it does give us a brilliant insight into the attitude of Jesus Christ toward woman, which itself has all the seeds of our present revolution of the rights and dignity of women. It will force the Church to reexamine this movement in light of the Gospels and not in the light of oppression of her own tradition and history. It will help the Church to become more truly herself as both man and woman make their fullest contribution to the Church precisely as man and woman in their proper dignity, equality, and genius.

The Church can no longer take for granted the male-dominated mentality which is a legacy of paganism, not of the gospels. In Christ, we have a model of womanly rights and dignity unexcelled by either Betty Friedan or Kate Millet.

X OBSCENITY

One of the greatest questions which has disturbed Catholics in particular over the years is the vast increase in the availability of pornographic materials. Over the years, the Catholic drives on "smut" 'have been proverbial, but it has never been scientifically shown that pornography induces healthy adults to any form of antisocial behavior. It would seem that the bone of contention would be exactly here, but this chapter will claim that it is not.

The real problem lies—as we have indicated at the very beginning of this book—in the Western world's inability to love correctly or, in short, to love at all. The large amount of pornography around today is a symptom—not a cause—of this profound malaise. The real problem of our society is not obscenity but the meaning and signification of love.

The theologian is often accused of obscuring his thought in professional jargon with the result that it is buried in "thematic" expressions. The question of language is, of course, a constant problem for the theologian, both in regard to the experience of God speaking and communicating to man, and in regard to the People of God to whom the theologian tries to communicate, in finite language, this same unchangeable message of God. It is a difficult task and that is why, I suppose, the theologian must resign himself to a life of tension between the past and the future in order to communicate with understanding and profit to the present. If he tries to break away from traditional modes of thought of the past because they have so little common experience with the present, he will be treated by many as a downright innovator—or worse!

Thus, it is with some trepidation that I approach the problem of censorship and obscenity, which clearly needs some rethinking in the modern day. So much has already been written on the subject that one hesitates to approach it again, and were it not for the fact that I was subpoenaed to appear in court in defense of a small poem called "The Love Book," I would not do so. Therefore, what follows may be called an "unthematized" theological reflection on the subject of obscenity for the Christian.

One's first reflection turns naturally to Scripture where we find interesting thoughts on the subject. One is from the Gospels:

> "Do you not see that whatever goes into a man from outside cannot defile him, since it enters, not his heart but his stomach, and so passes on?" And he said, "What comes out of a man is what defiles a man. For from within, out of the heart of a man, come evil thoughts, fornication, theft, murder, adultery, coveting, wickedness, deceit, licentiousness, envy, slander, pride, foolishness. All these evil things come from within, and they defile a man." (Mark 7, 18-23)

The message is clear: a man cannot be corrupted unless he *wishes* to be corrupted, for moral corruption comes from his heart which is essentially free. The morality of any action is in direct relationship to freedom, and without freedom there can be no morality, no morals. The ritualistic abstaining from "things" cannot make a man pure or impure; only the personal engagement of his responsible self can do this. Thus our first conclusion: the Christian, in his relationship to God and his brother, is essentially a free man who must respond in a free and loving way. No law, civil or canonical, can protect him from the absolute obligation to be free in his moral actions. Any law which impedes his freedom is no law but a robber of his most valuable possession as a man.

If we define obscenity in its broadest sense, we simply mean a desecration of the human person. That is, for our egotistical purposes, we treat a person as a means and not as an end. We have not seen in him a free agent, worthy of infinite love, in whom we can see our other selves, and even God. In the very act of loving my brother, I attain my brother. When we say that man's self-understanding occurs in the act of loving communication with a *thou*, we also affirm that in this act of love of neighbor the whole mystery of man is concentrated. We declare that all statements about man must be interpreted as statements about his love, which is the totality of his life. In love alone man comes to himself, encounters himself totally. He falls into the last abyss of his nature, his ultimate inability to grasp himself through reflection, the unfathomableness and risk of his existence, his hope and his despair, his lasting confrontation with a silent and absolute mystery surrounding his life, in which he ultimately finds himself, his brother, and his God in one and the same act of love. Thus the sacredness of this mystery of love, which is man and must be recognized if we are to understand the notion of obscenity. It is clear that when love is not present, we can "use" a human person sexually for our selfish purposes (even *within* marriage), but this is not the only—and indeed not the principal —form of desecration of the human person in modern society. Unfortunately, we have restricted the terminology to the sexual sphere, and this is a grave aberration. Is it not obscenity to enjoy vast wealth, luxuries of vertiginous variety, while millions starve to death each year and countless other human beings go to bed hungry every night? Is it not obscenity for the Christian to stand idly by while his government conducts a war in which it is conservatively estimated that for every soldier killed there are at least five civilians? Is it not obscenity to watch people so manipulated by TV commercials, propaganda, and a lying society that there is massive neurosis over the very meaning and significance of human life? Is not the violence inflicted on so many by the image of the TV screen and the vast militarism of our society a desecration of the human person and therefore an obscenity? Thus our second conclusion: modern society is insidiously corrupting man's dignity where these corruptions are accepted as the ubiquitous "American way of life" and where only abberations of the sexual sphere are singled out for castigation.

Why is this so? Simply because Western society has not been able to accept man's sexuality within the context of love; and sexuality without love is a prostitution of the human person. For various reasons—which we shall go into a moment—we have not been able to accept, let alone discuss, the human reality which is sexuality. It has been treated either as a "sacred" reality which one cannot discuss without candle and bell in hand, or as any other human function that one can engage in with no real effect on the existence of the person who engages in it. Both attitudes are vitiated by the fact that they disincarnate the reality of sexuality from its human context. Man *has* his sexuality, he *is* not his sexuality: it is a fundamental dynamism of the human person affecting him in his totality, and which must be used in the service of love, which is the whole mystery of man.

The Christian view of sexuality has been historically ambiguous. The biblical teaching is both blunt and beautiful. In Genesis I, 26-28 and 2, 18-24 we have the clear teaching that marriage is both an institution for the propagation of the human race as well as a mutual and loving relationship between a man and a woman. It is within this loving, sexually orientated relationship which is marriage that children are to be born as products of that love. Thus man as a sexual being is created in the image and likeness of God because he is a creator within and by love. Love and creation in the text of Genesis are essential if we are to understand the statement that man has been created in the image and likeness of God. In the New Testament (Eph. 5, 21-23) the sacred institution of marriage is elevated to a sacramental level in that this human love, already present from creation, is itself now made the symbol and efficacy of a greater reality, the love which continually exists between Christ and the Church. It is in the very act of loving in all of its human dimensions (which in marriage, includes above all as a sign of love, sexual relations) that the couple as a unit of love increase in their love of God. Sexuality in marriage is not "alongside of" the "spiritual" but an integral and essential part of the divine-human reality which is the sacrament of matrimony.

Yet, Western civilization has been infected by a crypto-Manichaeism or Gnosticism which has made matter—and above all sexual relationship—and evil, if not in fact, at least as a "grave temptation of the flesh." To the Christian spirit which sees all things as created and redeemed in Christ (John 1, 2-6), it should be evident that there is *nothing* which is evil—only what man by his perversity has made evil. When the Bible speaks of "flesh" it does not mean "matter"; it means simply man in his totality as a weak being completely dependent upon God for all things. To identify the biblical "flesh" with "matter" is to profess the very first Christian heresy against which our Creed reacted: "Creator of all things, visible and invisible." Indeed it was the theology of a St. Augustine on marriage which infected our moral views of this institution. It was taken up later in the sixteenth and seventeenth centuries by his faithful disciples, the Jansenists and Puritans. St. Augustine—who was never completely converted from Manichaeism which he professed as a young man —held every sexual act in marriage to be at least a venial sin since it involved the blinding passion of concupiscence. These attitudes have persisted in subtle ways in the Christian tradition, where even today most parents are incapable of imparting a proper sexual education to their children because it is somehow "shameful" to speak of these things openly and freely. And so they learn the facts of life" outside the context of love in the back rooms of school or in biology class—which are equally disastrous precisely because they are removed from the living example of love in the home. Of course, if this atmosphere of love is absent in the home, then we have all the ingredients of a potential disaster no matter how much these children know of the biological and psychological aspects of human sexuality.

Thus, many of our attitudes with regard to sexual functions have been corrupted by this subtle subterranean Manichaeism which is further compounded by the exploiters of sexuality in our commercial society. Never have Americans had so much manifestation of biological sexuality and never has there been so much deep unhappiness in our American society. We use the beautiful girl to sell everything from toothpaste to automobiles. This ought not to "shock" the Christian into reacting violently with: "There ought to be a law." There is vengeance as well as a crypto-homage in the fact that in both cases he agrees with what he is attacking, namely, manifestations of sexuality which are removed from love and are thereby degrading to the human person. This ought to be the source of the deepest sorrow for the Christian. He should see in it an indication that our society is deeply unhappy and trying to find escapes in *ersatz* methods of sex, alcohol, and drugs. Do police raids, crackdowns, more stringent obscenity laws, etc., really attack the heart of the problem? By no means. If the truth were known, they merely compound unhappiness by creating further dissension in society. This does not mean that no laws in this area are valuable. Certainly, adolescents ought to be protected from the exploiters of sexual emotion. But, outside of this very limited sphere, censorship laws are of doubtful moral validity. Since man is a free agent, he must be allowed to choose what he will or will not read—a responsibility that devolves on him, not someone else, even if, in fact, there are bound to be some individuals and publishers who are irresponsible. There is danger here, but the danger is intrinsic to the very notion of freedom. And here we have a further hangup: we are afraid of freedom. Politically and religiously we are afraid of freedom because it implies the terrible responsibility of making our own decisions and living according to our own consciences. At times, such freedom demands the agonizing decisions of a St. Thomas More (who remained faithful when all the bishops of England capitulated) or a Franz Jagerstatter (who opposed Hitler when all the Catholic bishops of Germany supported him). In reality, we do not trust people, so we must "have a law" or some institution "tell us what to do." Herein, of course, lies the whole crisis of authority as well as the present crisis of obscenity laws.

This brings us to my original reason for writing this chapter, namely, the small poem called "The Love Book." The principal objection to it has been that it uses four-letter words to describe human sexual activity in the service of the author's love. It's underlying ideas are basically good and theological: the total gift of love expressed in a thousand various ways of sexual manifestation which is incarnational. Yet, it is claimed that the words are offensive and therefore, the book must be banned. But the words are offensive because men have given them an offensive signification, not because they are "intrinsically evil."

The truth is that they are offended not by the words—for these same people use them from time to time—but by the fact that one author has had the courage to describe love incarnationally and humanly, something that both the "sacredizers" and the manipulators of the human reality of sexuality are incapable of understanding. The early Fathers of the Church and the Middle Ages were not so squeamish. In the Cathedral of Chartres (12th century) there is a very interesting tableau divided into two parts.

Its subject is the sacrament of matrimony, and the text is taken from the Epistle to the Ephesians 5:23, "Husbands, love your wives as Christ loved the Church." The first words above where we see the clear image of a Christian couple in bed in the evident act of sexual intercourse. Then the second frame has the words "as Christ loved the Church" over the clear image of Christ (with the divine halo) in bed with his wife, the Church, in the evident act of sexual embrace. Such an image is beautiful since it expresses so well—with little theological fanfare—the incarnational reality of human married love in its relation to Christ, the Incarnate Word. Once again, this would shock Christians today precisely because many of them are sexually sick. We must come back to the blunt understanding of human love incarnationally expressed in marriage. This emphasis was brought out by the *Constitution on the Church in the Modern World* of Vatican II where it made the following beautiful remark:

> This love is an eminently human one since it is directed from one person to another through an affection of the will; it involves the good of the whole person, and therefore can enrich the expressions of the body and the mind with a unique dignity, involving these expressions as special ingredients and signs of the friendship distinctive of marriage. This love God has judged worthy of special gifts, healing, perfecting, and exalting gift of grace and of charity. Such love, merging the human with the divine, leads the spouses to a free and mutual gift of themselves, a gift proving itself by gentle affection and by deed. . . . The actions within marriage by which the couple are united intimately and chastely are noble and worthy ones. Expressed in a manner which is truly human, these actions promote that mutual self-giving by which spouses enrich each other with a joyful and ready will (par. 49).

The text is a break from the subterranean Jansenism of the past and will do much to reorientate the sexual education of Christians. In reality, this is nothing new. We have a magnificent example in the *Song of Songs* of the Bible. The passages describe the intimate expression of incarnational love between man and woman.

Describing his-her beloved in a very erotic and symbolic manner, it expresses the incarnational nature of human love in a manner which would certainly be considered blasphemous by the "sacredizers."

> How graceful are your feet in sandals,
>> O queenly maiden!
> Your rounded thighs are like jewels,
>> The work of a master hand.
> Your navel is a rounded bowl
>> That never lacks mixed wine.
> Your belly is a heap of wheat,
>> encircled with lilies [genital area].
> Your two breasts are like two fawns,
>> Twins of a gazelle.
> Your neck is like an ivory tower.
> Your eyes are pools in Hesebon,
>> by the gate of Bathrabbin . . .
> How fair and pleasant you are
>> O loved one, delectable maiden!
> You are stately as a palm tree,
>> and your breasts are like its clusters.
> I say I will climb the palm tree
>> and lay hold of its branches (7:1-8).

This passage, properly translated, would never pass the censors of today and indeed some Christians have called for an "expurgated" version of the Bible. Thus, we see how deep is the sickness of sexuality in modern society, secular and religious, for both arrive at the same error but by different roads. The real problem of our society, then, is not obscenity but the meaning and signification of love in relation to its proper manifestation through the sexuality of the human person. For if we as Christians truly believe that loving our brother is ontologically identical with loving God (for it is the *same* act and reality of love in both cases) then first (at least in time and logically) we must understand and practice human love in all of its incarnational dimensions. This presupposes that we affirm—as Christianity must—the *oneness* of love of God and love of our brother, that we affirm that *only in this way* can we understand what God is and what Christ is, and only love God in Christ when we love the brother.

And to love the brother bears with it all the incarnational dimensions which we have mentioned. This is a mammoth task of Christian education which we have—with Vatican II—barely begun to communicate to the People of God. If Christians can only teach and practice among themselves the meaning and reality of love, we shall have made a positive contribution to curing society's sickness. In this view of Christian responsibility, obscenity laws will become as obsolete as Ford's Model T.

We shall then begin to communicate to the world not negative restraints but the *example* of incarnational, human love as is described for us so beautifully in the *Song of Songs:*

> Set me as a seal upon your heart,
>   as a seal upon your arm;
> for love is strong as death,
>   jealousy is cruel as the grave.
> Its flashes are flashes of fire,
>   a most vehement flame.
> Many waters cannot quench love,
>   neither can floods drown it.
> If a man offered for love
>   all the wealth of his house,
> it would be utterly as nothing (8, 6-7).